Endors

MW00985866

"Amping Your Abilities is a 'must have' reference guide for your spiritual library! Author Cynthia Singleton has created a heart-centered book for empaths and intuitives to explore and expand their natural psychic abilities. This book is easy to navigate and highly recommended for those awakening to their soul's purpose."

Alyson Gannon
Medium, Teacher and Best Selling Author
of The Last Breath

"This book feels like a wise friend that delivers a very personal, authentic, magical view into her life, as she guides you to your deepest, clearest, uplifting guidance. This book truly impacts your life in a positive awakened way, that brings out the best in you."

Dharma Cohen
Intuitive Healer, Former Sacred Guide to Mount
Shasta, Author of Calling All Orbs

"Want a delightful read with more than 75 processes for deepening your connection with the spiritual side of life? Cynthia Singleton's Amping Your Abilities: 77 Ways to Awaken, Explore, and Ignite Your Intuition is a wonderful collection of heartfelt stories and powerful processes. Her warm hearted curiosity and sense of play are evident in the personal anecdotes she shares in each chapter and her descriptions of the exercises are clear and concise. This book offers wisdom for those just beginning to explore these realms as well as for more seasoned explorers."

Nando Raynolds
MA, LPC, Psychotherapist, Martial Artist, and
Author

"Cynthia Singleton has crafted a delightfully welcoming book that invites going within to discover that there are many ways to explore intuition. She offers wonderful suggestions for experiencing the unfolding of joy and harmony. So much of what Cynthia conveys invites personal intuition, and that every moment—and person—in the now is a divine gift. The overall message I got was, trust the Universe...and myself!"

Michael Zanger
Author of Mount Shasta: History, Legends, and Lore.
Founder of Shasta Mountain Guides.

AMPING
YOUR
ABILITIES

77 Ways to Awaken, Explore,
and Ignite Your Intuition

CYNTHIA SINGLETON

ISBN Paperback: 978-1-952146-00-8
ISBN Electronic: 978-1-952146-01-5

Library of Congress Control Number: 2020901341

Portions of this book are works of nonfiction. Certain names and identifying characteristics have been changed.

Printed in the United States of America.

FRANKLIN ROSE
PUBLISHING

Franklin Rose Publishing
www.FranklinRose.com

Dedication

To Louie, who brings me Sunshine in exquisite ways. To my sister Kathleen, whose love has helped me conceptualize a glimpse of the size of the Universe. To Jonathan, whose generous wings spread a radiant light of playful grace and inquisitive inspiration. To my beloved Ashland community of loved ones—each of you! To the searching soul—you are not alone; for you travel with fellow explorers who collectively seek light and bring light.

Shine

Float in the Cosmos
Converse with beings

Believe in the magic
Of celestial things

The Power of Truth
Reveals itself

With jewels of sacred
And spiritual wealth

Fly beyond universe
And see through the veil

Believe in colors
While most see pale

Open your heart
Be brave, be seen

Emit your power
Share your gleam

Speak your tongue
Where once was shy

Shine your abilities
With arms to the sky

This spirit of yours
It is far, it is wide

Spread healing dust
For a world to abide

Cynthia Singleton

Foreword
by Jonathan Robinson

What you have before you may seem like an ordinary book, but it's really a description of portals to other worlds. In modern culture, we're bombarded with ads, social media, and news, but rarely informed about how to tap into the fantastic possibilities that lie within our deeper selves. This book offers you a full menu of methods for diving into the magic and mystery within. Unlike other books on intuition, it provides numerous secret keys, and it suggests you find the techniques that most call out to you.

I've had the honor of knowing the author, Cynthia, for enough time to know she is a true explorer of the inner realms. She brings a childlike wonder to life, and I've been inspired by her ability to walk her talk. As you'll soon find in this book, her open and explorative attitude is highly contagious. While you may think some of her suggestions are a bit unconventional, you may also be surprised to find that they truly work. Whether your goal is to better hear your intuition, or to further a spiritual awakening, you'll find plenty of great suggestions to help you along your path.

One of the things I loved about this book is that it doesn't advocate there is just one right way to connect with one's intuition and other miraculous abilities. Every person is unique, and therefore you must walk your own distinct path.

In a previous book I edited called, "The Experience of God," I interviewed 40 notable seekers such as the Dalai Lama, Ram Dass, Deepak Chopra, Byron Katie, Marianne Williamson, and many others. What I learned from such interviews is that each person must discover—through trial and error—what works to open up their own heart, intuition, and divine connection. With the many possibilities offered in this book, that task will be made much easier for you.

There are numerous advantages to getting better at amping your abilities. Of course, such a skill can be used to improve the quality of your decisions and your life. At the same time, I've noticed that people who consistently open up to their deeper potential make better partners, parents, friends, and even business associates. The ability to receive intuitive guidance and explore within will even make you a better citizen of the world. By amping your abilities, you'll be better able to serve your own higher self, the planet, and all those you love.

May you enjoy the journey....

Jonathan Robinson

Jonathan Robinson

Bestselling author of 14 books including,
"The Complete Idiot's Guide to Awakening Your Spirituality"
and "The Little Book of Big Questions."

Co-host of the podcast
"Awareness Explorers."

Table of Contents

Introduction

Have you ever felt afraid to express your intuitive abilities in the world? Can you relate to standing in front of another person and concealing your innate gifts? It wasn't that many years ago when the idea of intuitive voices held a societal stigma. It was as if psychic abilities were set aside to dark rooms and crystal balls. No wonder a good portion of us withdrew into hiding. Myself included.

Fortunately, those times are fading. Paradigms are shifting, and people are openly exploring their natural-born gifts. Intuitive talents are coming to light—out of the shadows. Intuition is like being in a world of gray that blossoms, instead, into a nuance of colors. Imagine if each of us were to tap into and share our innate abilities. Like a rain droplet on water, our intuitive gifts create ripples. Our own lives are impacted, as well as the world around us. As a lifetime teacher, I've held a trusted belief in the power of human potential. Humanity is awakening to intuitive amplification, and we are invited to participate!

> Imagine if each of us were to tap into and share our innate abilities. Like a rain droplet on water, our intuitive gifts create ripples.

With this book as your companion, enjoy the opportunity to nurture a healthy foundation for your innate gifts to flourish.

> This book is a bridge and a gateway—a compilation of tools for discovery and play!

> Whether coming out of hiding or choosing to shine brighter—enjoy the adventure to amplify your intuition!

Then further ignite your intuitive expansiveness with a multitude of activities. This book is a bridge and a gateway—a compilation of tools for discovery and play!

Sprinkled throughout are 77 numbered explorations located at the end of each chapter. Some activities may call to you more than others. That's okay! Use your intuition as your guide. Feel free to read from start to finish or choose a varied path. Whether coming out of hiding or choosing to shine brighter—enjoy the adventure to amplify your intuition!

May my lifetime journey of exploration inspire yours. Please join me for further discoveries at http://www.authorcynthia singleton.com.

Humanity is Awakening
to Intuitive Amplification

AuthorCynthiaSingleton.com

PART I

Setting the Foundation

Allowing

*There is nothing enlightened about shrinking so that other people won't feel insecure around you.
We are all meant to shine...*
—Marianne Williamson

As a young girl, I remember sitting on the floor in the occult section of the library stacks on bended knee. I was utterly absorbed in material about all things unknown. I recall shyly peering from left to right, hoping no one would see me in the occult section. I was afraid I might get caught. "Caught?" What did that mean to me, "get caught?" I'm not entirely sure. Perhaps it was a past life experience— burned at the stake? Maybe it was a concern of being judged or ridiculed. Why was I afraid to feel comfortable in the light of these incredibly fascinating subjects? Despite my fear, I found an absolute thrill to discover the world as we did or didn't see it. Can you relate?

At my deepest core, I held an interest in subjects like ghosts, UFOs, mysterious creatures, psychic studies, astrology, angels, superstition, and magic. What was real? What wasn't? What could be a figment of imagination? My quest for "possibility" has been a lifetime endeavor. And not always publicly. I was selective to whom I might reveal this interest or share these conversations a matter of years ago.

Over time, however, I've become increasingly transparent in my enthusiasm for things unknown. In my lifetime, I've witnessed pioneering individuals break ground. Medical professionals are stepping up to share their accounts of patients' near death experiences (NDE's). Dr. Raymond Moody, who coined the term, has gathered extensive NDE resources and testimonies. Public figures are going on record about their experiences with ghosts and spirits. Shows such as *Hollywood Medium with Tyler Henry* have celebrities supporting mediumship skills. Psychotherapists and hypnotherapists have explored past lives and in-between lives. The Newton Institute, with a worldwide scope of credentialed therapists, investigates such findings. The scientific community is further examining consciousness— our existence beyond physical matter. Intuitive explorations are finally becoming mainstream. I'm not alone in a fascination for "things unknown." Thank goodness.

The following exercises helped me to step further from my quiet comfort zone. They've built a foundation in my desire to shine an authentic light in the world.

Recently, a dear friend of mine pointed out that when he shares a miraculous story, people have something extraordinary to share in return. I'm finding this to be true—that a magical door can be opened. Sure, with some audiences, I choose these conversations carefully. I find that people generally seem eager to exchange amazing experiences—even if they are looking over their shoulders. What miraculous stories do you have to tell?

If you're anything like me, I'm learning to explore these realms, unhidden. You're invited to do the same. The following exercises helped me to step further from my quiet comfort zone. They've built a foundation in my desire to shine an authentic light in the world.

1. **Exploration—Written Proclamation**

   Not long after synchronicity brought me to the town of my dreams—I came across a proclamation. It was on a sticky note. I'd written it not long before my transformative move to Ashland, Oregon. The words said, "I claim my place in creation." To this day, that note is posted inside my bathroom cabinet. Now and again, I proclaim those words with conviction. What's your desire? Try writing a statement that resonates with your purest wishes. Write it as if it has transpired. Then, read it daily. *Feel* your proclamation with intention. For less than one minute of daily practice, you may see your world shift entirely. As I did—I'm now living in a town that feels like home.

2. **Exploration—Tapping**

   Tapping, also known as Emotional Freedom Technique (EFT), was developed by Gary Craig, a Stanford graduate with a lifetime interest in the impacts of thoughts on healing. Tapping ties into the premise of ancient eastern health practices. Similar to acupuncture, meridians (or energy centers) of the body can transform states of being. Initially, I was skeptical—until I worked with an EFT practitioner and experienced the benefits myself. When I tap into meridian points on my body, I use affirming statements to ignite transformation. After calling 911 to report a fire, I once tapped, "Even though I feel scared, I am safe." As a life goal, I've used phrases such as, "I'm a beautiful soul, ready to shine my trusting light for the greater good of humanity." What would suit you?

Tapping tutorials can be easily retrieved, for free, from reputable sources online. Enter "Tapping" or "EFT" into your online search box and see which resources resonate with you.

3. **Exploration—Mirror Exercises**

    Mirror exercises provide a powerful mechanism to shift one's perception. I once worked with a healing practitioner who prescribed mirror exercises for 30 days. It was after a traumatic breakup, and I was feeling uncertain about my life's next steps. Over time, I noticed a significantly improved shift in my optimism and groundedness. To this day, I continue to do mirror exercises.

    You can practice the following while looking into your eyes in the mirror. You might feel resistant at first. I certainly did—so I encourage you to persevere. Choose meaningful words to say to yourself with compassion and conviction. Below are examples of mirror exercises. Feel free to use these or write your own. State them as if they've magnificently transpired:

    - "I let go and trust that life is perfectly timed and miraculous."
    - "I invite and allow unlimited abundance into every aspect of my life."
    - "I demonstrate loving action every day."
    - "I allow my valuable intuitive contributions to flourish."

Summary

Building a foundation of "allowing" welcomes miraculousness.

Exploring intuitive practices is a good way to enhance the world we live in. Tapping and mirror exercises are ways to awaken potential. Building a foundation of "allowing" welcomes miraculousness. I feel elated when I imagine a world full of people stepping into the light to embrace their gifts.

Stepping into Gratitude

> *It is through gratitude for the present moment that the spiritual dimension of life opens up.*
> **—Eckhart Tolle**

When in your darkest moments, what pulled you through? In my dark days, I found a powerful spark—gratitude. Gratitude is like a life raft—it keeps us afloat on stormy seas.

While my young childhood years were full of mystery and awe, my teenage years were another story. My early years included family outings and playful romping with my dad, mom, and older sister. Walking nature trails, building sandcastles, and family belly laughter filled my younger days. Yet, things changed when my family left the southern California coast to move to the opposite end of the state. My father's job was stressful. My basic needs were met, yet my parents were consumed with responsibilities. Their marriage strained, and my once-Prince-Charming father turned to alcohol.

When I felt overwhelmed, nature was my escape. I would look at the beauty of the hillsides or contemplate dancing sparkles on waters. I covered my bedroom walls with images of tranquil tropical locations. Toxic moments, including living with an agitated alcoholic father, were outshined by finding the things that glimmered good, which brought gratitude. What have been your rays of light in tough times?

In my life travels, I discovered the value of inner exploration. I explored self-help books and followed interests in things unknown. Yes, I was a kid who practiced telekinesis with thumbtacks on my childhood bed. I'd flip red and black playing cards to challenge my ESP skills. Outdoors, the night sky intrigued me as I contemplated life on other planets. An entire world could be explored by exploring from within. Did you also delve into inward escapes?

Over time, I realized that one thing was certain—life is not predictable. Chaos is inevitable. Like many, I know about curling up on the kitchen floor after a tender breakup. The death of loved ones introduced me to sofa-bound dark days. There's nothing like a good scream in the car to release anger or sadness. Grieving, without resistance, allows emotions to wash through me. It also allows me to move into a place of acceptance—with an opportunity to heal.

> The Universe steers our course, and I hope to recognize the positive gifts along the way.

In those difficult times, I could choose to fixate on lack or victimhood. Naturally, I've had my share of those thoughts. Yet, when moving through tough experiences, I've found I function much better when choosing gratitude. I look for gifts in what life brings—even if life doesn't turn out as expected. The Universe steers our course, and I hope to recognize the positive gifts along the way.

In gratitude, I find peace and comfort, providing an opening to tap into intuition's clarity. My energetic vibration is raised.

In that, I can better sense miraculousness—like recognizing the
vibration of a thriving flower. Or
feeling the elation of a dog's
happiness. Gratitude shifts our

> Gratitude shifts our state
> of being into a place of
> reception and openness.

state of being into a place of reception and openness.

Let's play with the following activities. Notice how you feel
before the exercises and then tune in to how you feel once
you've completed them:

4. **Exploration—Gratitude Activity**
    Consider three things for which you feel grateful. As
    some examples, I feel thankful for my playful cat,
    Sunshine. Writing brings me joy. The trees outside
    my window bring me peace. Take a moment to look
    around. Close your eyes (after reading this!) and think
    of things that bring you gratitude. There may be times
    it's hard to find gratitude. On those days, choose
    something as simple as appreciation for having oxygen
    to breathe. Use each of your senses and dive into the
    positive emotions associated with the three things
    which help you feel grateful. Bathe in the experience
    for a minute or more.

You can practice this gratitude activity upon waking,
throughout the day, at bedtime, or even when you step
into the bathroom. This exercise is a foundational tool
to fine-tune your awareness to a state of high vibration.
Like me, you might discover that practicing gratitude
can become addictive when immersing in this elevated
state. Energy and resources are charging rather than
depleting. Gratitude can sharpen and hone powerful,
intuitive abilities.

5. Exploration—Celebrating Gratitude

I feel delighted when meeting with a friend and sharing the things for which we feel grateful. How about lifting your spirits with a gratitude date? On your own or with a friend, set aside a specific time on your calendar. Show up with an appreciation for all things, "gratitude." Enjoy snacks or beverages and bring a list of ideas for which you are grateful. Light a candle or blow bubbles. What's a song or poem that ignites your feelings of gratitude? Share and immerse in sheer appreciation.

6. Exploration—Mental Picture of the Day

Be on the lookout for something that moves you in your daily living. Is it the way the light shines on leaves in nature? How about witnessing a kind deed, such as someone opening the door for another person? Or seeing a dog's nose against a car window? When you feel that moment of awe, take a mental snapshot. My goal is to take one mental picture a day. Over time, this activity has reinforced me to recognize great depths of beauty in our world. Finding visual authenticity in each day lifts my vibration of gratitude.

Summary

> Gratitude is a lifeline in this world's chaos.

Gratitude is a lifeline in this world's chaos. It invites a positive foundation from which to approach life. Energetic reserves are ignited when tapping into higher vibrations. It lifts our intuition.

What's Your Magnitude
of Gratitude?

AuthorCynthiaSingleton.com

Self-Care

Though I generally live a healthy lifestyle, I can relate to scrumptious temptation. Sweets are my kryptonite—especially chocolate ones. Resisting a mass-market chocolate-rolled pastry was one of my New Year's resolutions. Buttery, cheesy mashed potatoes (with bacon) is one of my favorite comfort foods. I know about indulging in that extra glass of wine after a hard day. And yet, I ask myself—do I ultimately feel better when emotionally indulging? In the devouring process, yes. But after contemplation, no. What's your temptation?

While I believe (and partake) in occasional splurging when in a state of stress, compounding my uncomfortable experiences with additional oblivion hasn't served me well.

When the Covid-19 pandemic landed in the United States, it first hit my sister's region of Washington state. There were tumultuous unknowns. I read debatable news articles, and I sifted through polarized threads on social media. As many people were, I was feeling discombobulated with the onset of pandemic news.

A few weeks into the pandemic, a friend in mutual isolation came to visit me. I hadn't realized how much bewilderment I was experiencing until his visit. I saw myself acting fidgety. It seemed that once I sat down for a conversation, I was back up to attend to some little detail like opening a window or getting a drink of water. I was aware of feeling relentlessly hungry. I felt a consuming desire to "be comfortable" as the world was in a heightened state of discomfort.

Coincidentally, this friend and I enjoy diving into awareness explorations. During his visit, I realized I wasn't bringing my optimal intuitiveness into the room. I wasn't connecting to my highest self in my usual way. Ultimately, seeing myself in his presence offered self-awareness. I could benefit from self-care. As the pandemic spread, keeping my body in good health ringed of great importance. My emotional state could use loving-care too.

> When taking care of foundational needs, our capacity to call upon intuition heightens.

Think of times when you could have used more self-care. Can you relate to that hazy, unfocused feeling? When taking care of foundational needs, our capacity to call upon intuition heightens. It's like putting on an oxygen mask, first, in a flight emergency. We can function better when we've attended to our basic needs.

The following are ways to nurture self-care—especially in times of stress. Having these tools on hand can prevent a need to rack your brain for ideas when you feel vulnerable. If you have significant needs, please seek a qualified professional.

7. Exploration—Self-Care Considerations

Prepare a list you can put in a special place for you to access. Fill in the blanks below. It may take time to develop this list, but think of building it as a ritual of sorts. I recommend writing out all answers even if they don't initially seem relevant. Avoiding answers may heighten our awareness to places of need. If you make a digital copy, I recommend printing your list and holding it when needed. Doing so can be like a sacred act in and of itself:

- My ideal amount of sleep per 24 hours is...
- My favorite way of getting beneficial exercise is...
- I feel happy when I practice activities such as...
- Healthy snacks and foods I especially like are...
- The amount of water I aim to drink each day is...
- Parts of myself that can use self-love are...
- A primary need of which I could seek self, group, or professional support is...
- The ideal number of minutes per day I could meditate solely on gratitude is…

As examples, my answers are below:

- My ideal amount of sleep per 24 hours is *7 to 9 hours*
- My favorite way of getting beneficial exercise is *to walk and to dance*
- I feel happy when I practice activities such as *playing with my pet*
- Healthy snacks and foods I especially like are *protein bars and avocados*
- The amount of water I aim to drink each day is *8 to 10 glasses*
- Parts of myself that can use self-love are *the parts that feel abandoned by my father*
- A primary need of which I could seek self, group, or professional support is *to occasional check-in on my overall wellbeing or in times of crisis*
- The ideal amount of minutes per day I could meditate solely on gratitude is *ten minutes a day*

As you complete this self-care exercise, consider what feeds your energy. What's optimal for you? You probably won't tackle all of these at all times. The idea is to build intuitive capacity—by emerging from a foundation of wellness.

8. Exploration—Self-Care Magnification

> Our inner journey ignites a dance with our outer world.

To amplify the idea of self-care, how about further magnifying your spirit? Our inner journey ignites a dance with our outer world. Go deeper and enjoy the following to help you thrive:

- Beautiful images of which I can meditate or call upon are...
- Songs, artists, or genres of music that feel vibrant to me are...
- My favorite places in nature are...
- Geographical locations I can easily travel to where I experience peace are…
- Pleasant places I could read a book or meditate are...
- Places I can soak or bathe to "cleanse my soul" are…
- Ideas of places to walk are...
- Three of my favorite feel-good words I can focus on are…

As examples, my answers are below:

- Beautiful images of which I can meditate or call upon are *tropical settings and mountain scenery*
- Songs, artists, or genres of music that feel vibrant to me are *Vivaldi, 80's music, tribal sounds, Sarah Brightman*
- My favorite places in nature are *near oceans, lakes, and streams*
- Geographical locations I can easily travel to where I experience peace are *local parks or the coast*
- Places I can soak or bathe to "cleanse my soul" are *in my bathtub or mineral springs*
- Pleasant places I could read a book or meditate are *at the park or on my perch (porch)*
- Ideas of places to walk are *on a local trail or in a nearby neighborhood*
- Three of my favorite feel-good words I can focus on are *love, playfulness, and bliss*

9. Exploration—Namaste Statement

Another technique to drop into high vibration is to write what I call a "namaste statement." What brings you peace? As I understand it, Namaste in Sanskrit basically means, "I bow to you." I've often heard the modern use of Namaste to mean that the peace in me honors the peace in you. What if everyone approached the world this way?

A Namaste Statement might say something like, "The bliss in me honors the bliss in you." Or, "The happiness in me brings happiness to the world." Your Namaste Statement can be a guiding focus. You can use it at the gym or at work. How about calling upon it in stressful situations, such as when in traffic?

In review, here's a template to create your own Namaste Statement:

The (emotion) in me (action word) the (same emotion) in (you, others, or the world).
Examples:
The joy in me honors the joy in you.
The peacefulness in me appreciates the peacefulness in others.

As you begin writing your Namaste Statement, you might realize that something meaningful arises. Listen to your intuition as you create your Namaste Statement. Place this statement in a preferred place where you can read it now and again.

10. Exploration—Laughter

Has it been too long since your last belly laugh? An excellent way to promote wellness is to let ourselves be filled with laughter. Elevate your mood with intentional laughter. Tune into a comedy, explore animal antics on the Internet, or read uplifting articles. Enjoy podcasts, listen to comedians, or reminisce funny stories with loved ones. Watch your pets play or go to a dog park. Explore what works for you.

Experience release and bring intentional laughter into your presence.

Summary

Self-care is like
foundational nutrients
in a garden.

When we nurture the
vessel that holds our
energetic body, we
magnify our spirit!

Self-care is like foundational nutrients in a garden. It improves our wellbeing, which benefits our loved ones too. Our ability to tap into intuitive capacity is increased when we exercise self-care. When we nurture the vessel that holds our energetic body, we magnify our spirit!

Love

I've found that love in its purest form is Divine—it gives, it dances, and it plays! It offers vast potential in the quality of our lives. How about stepping into that? I'm in my highest state when in the vibration of love. When my cat, Sunshine, and I chase one another around our home, I feel elated. When dancing with friends, I experience a heightened state of bliss. I see love when gazing into a beloved's sparkling eyes. Where do you experience your highest states of love?

Love is a catalyst for a higher state of awareness—it transmits well-beingness and supports intuition. It helps me feel connected to a sense of knowingness. It reaches beyond the scope of everyday life—to my highest self. Love carries us past the threshold of logic: in a whisper, a calling, or a nudge.

Not long ago, I had a cat who played a role in my intuitive development. A cat? Yes. "How?" you

> Love is a catalyst for a higher state of awareness—it transmits well-beingness and supports intuition.

> Love carries us past the threshold of logic: in a whisper, a calling, or a nudge.

23

might ask. With love. Louie Dewey Mocha Latte is the soul you see pictured on the spine of this book. A magnificent being—we shared an incredibly blissful journey.

Have you known a pet to transform your life? Louie was there when my life took an unexpected turn. Following a life-altering slip on ice, his love carried me into a new journey. My active life of skiing and mountain biking made an about-face. For some time, I could hardly walk around the block due to my injuries. I went from an outdoorsy athlete to, instead, channeling my writing passions. In support, Louie sat beside me day after day. He was my comfort and companion. This loving cat kept my spirits high as "pen flowed to paper."

Despite the so-called tragedy, my intuitional endeavors flourished while feeling the loving presence of this cat. My energies were directed into creating. There was synchronicity in meeting tragedy with love. Over the next few years, my first books came together, with ease—with Louie as my helper.

Love raises our vibration and heightens our energetic wellness. Recognizing and compounding it provides a foundation for intuition to thrive. The following are ways to elevate our loving experiences:

11. Exploration—Magnificent Being
When one on one with another person, imagine them as the most important person of that moment. With healthy boundaries, give that person 100% of your focus. Practice "being in the sacred now." Celebrate their pure essence of love. When I've gone to my dance classes, I've imagined that the individual dancing across from me is a Divine gift—precisely the most important person on the planet. Connecting to the sacredness in others heightens the capacity for

24

intuitive awareness. This can be done in a variety of settings and scenarios.

As related, the Universe might surprise you. Long ago, I was at a post-mountain bike gathering. In a dining pub, our large group ran out of table room. I wound up sitting at a separate table with a visiting stranger who had joined us on our ride. Initially, I was disappointed to be apart from our group. Yet, when giving this man my full interest, I found out that he had been in one of the Twin Towers on September 11th, 2001. His 911 story was an opportunity not only to feel magnificently connected to this man—but also to experience greater love for humanity.

12. Exploration—Nurturing Your Pet

Have you ever felt pure elation when a kitten makes acrobatic Matrix-like aerial feats in the air? Has your dog ever melted you with a single look? Take the extra time to nurture your pet with your complete and playful attention. I believe our pets are teachers and soul mates. Brush them, nurture them, send them your loving energy. Lounge with them, talk to them. Perhaps even sing to them or dance. I've had pets who enjoyed engaging in song and dance. Play and frolic—watch their body language to get feedback on what they like most. Being on the floor with them may produce a blissful belly stretch. Immerse in love by setting aside intentional time for your pets. Offering a nurturing connection is a way to increase your loving vibration.

13. Exploration—Immerse With Your Children

As a child, did you ever feel a tremendous desire to be seen and heard? When I was young, I remember those lonely moments when the adult world seemed too preoccupied to notice me. With years of experience as an elementary school teacher, I've seen students thrive when given undivided attention. If you have kids, think about how often you offer them your full focus. Kids can be confused, at first, when you unexpectedly increase your attention. Persevere—even if your love doesn't initially feel received. Go for a walk, share a meal, or ask about the things that bring them happiness. Listen actively. Embrace their quirks and share what you love about them. What lessons have they've taught you? Children might be less apt to find less attractive ways to vie for attention when feeling seen and heard. You may even free up energy by being proactive about giving undivided love to children.

14. Exploration—Energetic Love

Have you ever been in a room where the tension was high, or the energy felt "off?" Perhaps you've been with an acquaintance and couldn't get a word in edgewise. If pressures elevate with a person or situation, you can try shifting a room's vibration. The first time I tried this, when it was difficult for me to speak or interact, I practiced filling the room with unconditional energetic love.

As if love were rising water, I imagined filling the room from floor to ceiling. I was pleasantly surprised because I felt an almost immediate shift. The person relaxed and gave me space to speak. It's not up to you to control the "temperature" of a room or person, yet this can be a fun thing to play with to see if you can ignite results.

15. Exploration—A Day of Unconditional Love

Try going through a day of giving only love. Acknowledge and appreciate all that shows up. Give the spotlight to others with your full attention. Actively listen and share words of affirmation. Offer quality time or assistance. Be the loving part of yourself that can devote to the pure act of giving. Do not practice this to get anything back. Try it multiple times and observe. Then gather evidence of the impact of your loving abilities. The 2013 movie, *About Time,* has a scene about living the same day, twice. One day is lived monotonously. The same day, lived again, is played out with intentional love. I hope to remember to do the latter.

Now, offer yourself a well-deserved day of unconditional love. Listen to your needs. Offer yourself affirming thoughts, such as, "I like how I am compassionate to others." Or, "I love how I adore nature." Acknowledge your acts and deeds throughout the day. Take time to immerse yourself in what brings joy, like preparing a delicious meal or walking in the park. Let go of social programming that may hint at loving yourself as being selfish. Permit yourself to fill your energetic reserves with time, love, and appreciation. Your replenished love-tank benefits others in your world.

Summary

Love is of the highest essence—it illuminates our everyday path. Our intuition thrives in this catalyzing vibration. Love promotes the capacity for our innate abilities to unfold. Sharing your loving gifts with yourself and others makes the world shine that much brighter!

> Love is of the highest essence—it illuminates our everyday path. Our intuition thrives in this catalyzing vibration.

Space and Place
for Sacred Practices

Take a look around your home. Is there an area or space to enhance your intuitive practices? My body takes a peaceful breath when I reflect on the sacred space I've created in my home. I appreciate the sunlit setting with soft pillows, fuzzy throw blankets, and outdoor photography. My nearby altar is adorned with semi-precious stones and white candles. Creative thought and energetic practices are nurtured in my space. How about you? Do you have a meaningful space to nurture *you*?

I find the word "sacred" to mean something extraordinarily meaningful. For some, sacred refers to God, Spirit, or holiness. For others, it means peace from the chaos of everyday routines. To amplify a sense of sacredness in your space, let's explore your home through new eyes. Even if well-versed in sacred surroundings, I invite you to evaluate your home via a fresh lens.

When you look around your living space, do you notice particular colors that inspire happiness and tranquility? Are you able to move about freely, or do you trip on "to do's?" Do you have places to set aside the distraction of clutter, papers, and bills? Which areas are you drawn to and why?

Take a walk-through. What in your surroundings supports peace and joy? What ignites a sense of inner vitality? Do particular spaces or images help you to feel open and expansive?

> Creating sacred space in our home offers the opportunity to focus, channel, and play with energetic possibilities.

Creating sacred space in our home offers the opportunity to focus, channel, and play with energetic possibilities. As you enhance your home, you might realize that your choices are either limited or endless. Whether you have a small corner or large open space, you can create a tranquil environment for your practices. Where might you create an energetically harmonious atmosphere?

The following are considerations in creating your sacred space:

- Find a place free of bills, clutter, and chaos.
- Locate space for you alone.
- Bring in favorite colors, textures, or images.
- Set up inspirational items. What lifts your spirits?
- How about photographs or statuettes?
- Do you like special lighting?
- An instrument or Tibetan bowl can feel welcoming.
- Do you want a flat surface space for activities such as Tarot spreads?

The following are ways to enhance your space further:

16. Exploration—An Altar for Energetic Practice

An altar is a table or flat area where meaningful items are placed. It's a space to deepen and further your intuitive practices. Candles, cherished photographs, journals, spiritual artifacts, and crystals are examples of what one might place on an altar. What suits you? Choose a surface to place things that honor your beliefs, purposes, and intentions. I've chosen an antique desk next to my bedside. If you don't already have an altar, a table, a box, or a console will do. If you'd like, cover it with a tablecloth, sarong, or placemat. Now decide if you want to have a comfy place to sit next to your altar. Your space can be a place to meditate, contemplate, and create with sacred intention.

17. Exploration—Journaling

Keep a journal in your space to let your thoughts flow. Reflect on the ideas listed below and tap into your intuition—and tune into what feels inspiring to you.

Here are some starters:

- Write about a wish you'd like to manifest
- Journal about miraculous events you've encountered in your life
- Capture triumphant memories that inspired or moved you
- Put into words, the intuitive abilities you hope to enhance or explore
- Document intuitive experiences and discoveries

18. Exploration—Music and Poetry

Music is vibrational. In turn, what vibration improves your state of being? How about playing inspiring music? As I write this, river sounds are playing in the background from the Internet. It helps me feel open and tranquil. For fun, try making a meal to a playlist of happy songs. Or contemplate the beauty of life to Louis Armstrong singing, *What a Wonderful World*. Play a variety of music to see what lifts you.

Like music, poetry is an intentional source of inspiration. Explore uplifting poems or write your own. I have self-written poetry framed throughout my home. I occasionally read these poems out loud for fun. They help me feel connected to the things that heighten the nature of my intuition.

19. Exploration—Trinkets or Natural Artifacts

You may already have items in your home or on your altar that feel sacred to you. Perhaps you have trinkets from trips you've taken. Is there a meaningful object that brings a smile? Seashells, travel souvenirs, and semi-precious stones adorn my home. Every so often, I choose a treasured item and hold it to my chest. Clasping a shell stimulates my senses to ocean memories. Holding certain rocks can help me feel grounded. Give it a try.

20. Exploration—Pendulum Work

I keep a pendulum at my altar. A pendulum is often a stone or a crystal suspended from a string or a chain. It's used to tap into one's higher self for answers. I feel I'm tuning into Divine when using my pendulum. You can first calibrate a pendulum's swing by confirming your name. For example, I would ask, "Is my name, Cynthia Singleton?" Yes, and no directions might be different for each person—my pendulum swings in a circle for yes while back and forth means no. When using my pendulum, I begin by stating its use is only to be for my highest good. I also imagine surrounding myself with Divine white light.

Over time, my pendulum has revealed precise insights. One example is learning the specific day I would find my current kitty cat. I'd been on the lookout for nearly a year. Months before I got my kitten, Sunshine, I narrowed down the exact date I'd find her by asking yes and no calendar-related questions. Another example of pendulum answers was when I learned my stepdad had severe symptoms that took him to the emergency room. My pendulum revealed his condition was not as critical as first thought. After an overnight stay in the hospital and a series of tests, he was discharged the next day.

It is worthy to note that my pendulum has not always granted answers. It will swing a substantial "no" when I'm not to know the answer. It's shown both yes and no, simultaneously, when something is not to be revealed. It swings randomly when the inquiry is for someone else—to ask of themselves.

21. Exploration—Automatic Writing

Automatic writing is another way to tune into insight from your higher self and Divine. Keep a sketchbook or journal. I find it most comfortable to connect when I am in a location with minimal distractions.

I start by calling in Divine intention to surround me for the benefit of my highest good. Next, I ask a question and wait for words to flow onto paper. I write what randomly pops into my head. Don't overthink it. Let it flow.

I've almost set the pen down when attempting to decipher what was flowing out. Messages don't often make sense until entirely written, which is an excellent reminder to keep thoughts out of the process. Breathe, relax, and be a witness.

To see what works best for you, you can try automatic writing in a non-dominant hand. Keep in mind that the written messages may not relate to your question. Not all inquiries will be given answers. I feel this is because Spirit encourages us to act on our free-will. When automatic writing for my best and highest good, I've only experienced messages of love and supportive insight.

22. Exploration—Crystals

If quartz crystals can help to regulate certain electronics, I wonder how crystals impact our energy field. A friend introduced me to holding stones against my solar plexus area—between my lower ribs. To try, close your eyes and feel your general emotion when holding each crystal. Compare your impressions when feeling into each one separately. When purchasing crystals, some people mentally ask for guidance on if the stones have a quality that can be of service.

Sacred stones can be charged in sunlight for a day. They can also be energetically purified by setting them on earth or dirt overnight. Some like to energize their crystals in the moonlight. Try what feels right to you. I experience unique vibrations from some of my favorite stones:

- Amethyst: peaceful tranquility
- Rose quartz: loving-kindness
- Healerite: healing joy
- Obsidian or Tourmaline: powerful protection
- Tiger's Eye: courageous perseverance
- Garnet: true love
- Moonstone: magical encouragement

Summary

Sacred space invites your intuition to be nurtured. Enrich a personal sanctuary to grow your gifts—a place to rejuvenate and transform your abilities. Customize your energetic retreat. What feels supportive—music, poetry, artifacts, and crystals? Revitalize and experiment—this is *your* hallowed ground!

Sacred space invites your intuition to be nurtured. Enrich a personal sanctuary to grow your gifts—a place to rejuvenate and transform your abilities.

Passion, Creativity, and Flow

> *Passion is energy. Feel the power that comes from focusing on what excites you.*
> **—Oprah Winfrey**

What ignites you? What excites you? When my attention is on passion, creativity, and flow, my energy amplifies. As a child, my sister and I often played outside. I remember being called to dinner when it felt like we had just started! Can you think of a time when you were so absorbed, you lost all sense of time?

For me, writing is one of my happiest satisfactions. I've had plenty of evenings when it dawned on me that I had written for hours. These are moments I realize the only light in my home is emanating from my computer. When completely absorbed, I've been asked, "Have you eaten today?" It's been amusing to realize a cup of tea or a piece of chocolate was sitting beside me for hours, untouched. I find immense pleasure in writing—often feeling like words are channeling.

Photography does the same for me. I've been on magnificent wintery photoshoots when I realized, only later, that I'd chilled myself to the bone. Immersed, I'd been mesmerized by visual miracles, like frozen spider webs and frosty leaves.

Perhaps this is key to passion, creativity, and flow—it brings us into the moment, like an artist who drops into the imagery of shadow and light. Like mountain bikers, kayakers, and skiers. When active, they have little room for outside thoughts.

> One of our highest states of being is when we're in what brings us present joy.

Have you ever approached a young child who was absorbed in play? Kids are masters at drawing us into a whole world of creativity, dimension, and imagination! It's no wonder a child sometimes melts down when stepping out of play. One of our highest states of being is when we're in what brings us present joy. We are in the flow of our soul.

When in nature, have you ever watched the light dance on water? How about listening to the sound of dragonflies in aerial feats? Or bees zipping through fauna? Have you been in awe of purple skies with mountain silhouettes at dusk? You might sense my love for nature, poetry, and photography. In it, I lose all sense of time and space—where my intuition is alive.

> When I am in my full presence of passion, I can sense the signature vibration of each marvel in nature.

I had a memorable moment with one of my friends. He drew my attention to the shaking leaves outside of his window. Autumn aspen leaves shimmered like confetti on nature's breath. I felt suspended in time as we shared this majestic observation. Taking in the sights, sounds, and sensations in life fine-tune our senses. It channels our energy and drops us into the present moment. When I am in my full presence of passion, I can sense the signature vibration of each marvel in nature. My first self-published book of poetry and photography is called *Nature Speaks*. When I'm in my highest receptive state of natural wonders, it feels like nature does speak!

Where do you like to focus your energy? What playful activities ignite your "Yes?"

When we step into flow—it kindles our passion. We ignite our unique spark in the world that can ultimately serve others. I find great joy and flow as a poet, photographer, and writer. In

> Accentuate the magnitude of creativity and passion. When channeled— what a force!

contrast, I have a friend who's gifted at repairing computers. A florist, a fisherman (or woman), a real estate agent, a veterinarian, a geologist, a firefighter—each have skills, passions, and strengths to bring to the world. Please do not misinterpret these examples as only a status of accomplishment. Accentuate the magnitude of creativity and passion. When channeled—what a force!

I encourage you to listen to your intuition as you engage in the following activities. Where does your energy flow? You might find the Universe is nudging your direction:

23. Exploration—Discovery of Passions

Write a list of what you love to do. Don't think—write. I used to prompt my elementary school students to let their thoughts out. To, at first, not get caught up in details or grammar. We'd sing a quick reminder to the tune of a familiar holiday song, "Let it flow, let it flow, let it flow." Editing could come later. The point was not to let overthinking get in the way.

No need to complicate the flow of what arises—put words to paper for about ten minutes. What excites you? When completing this session, circle words that stand out—you might discover a pattern. See what draws you into the flow of creativity. You might find something unexpected! Doing more of what you love supports your natural intuition. If you're anything like me, you might genuinely enjoy this writing exercise and wind up writing a book—or few!

24. Exploration—Lost Time

Think back to times you were utterly absorbed in feeling a happy, high vibration. What sorts of activities were you doing when you lost track of time? Recall a variety of interests throughout your life and make a note of these experiences. Write a list, and over the next few months, playfully explore similar opportunities. Expand into the innate joy of your nature!

25. Exploration—Play and Movement

Speaking of play, try it. I was a facilitator at a workshop where we gave adults time to go outside and play. Given time, they loved it! Find a location where you can be yourself, unbarred. Skip, hum, sing, listen, dig, build, imagine, or solve. At first, you might feel shy or self-judgemental. Experiment. Recognize what brings laughter and bliss. Consider trying this activity with your kids or pets. If you don't have your own, how about a playdate with friends and their kids? Dogs are a great example of romping freely! A guru of frolicking—dogs, are an instant playmate!

Draw out what ignites positive feelings inside of you. An intuitive friend of mine once gave me a "reading," stating that dance serves my soul. I agree—dance

40

is my "yes!" It releases my energetic, physical, and emotional blockages. It also ignites my experiences with passion, creativity, and flow.

Summary

What enlivens you? What feels innate and natural? Channeling into the flow of our passions is a worthy endeavor—it taps us into our best self. Creativity is the seed through which the soul can express itself—bring *yours* to the world!

> Channeling into the flow of our passions is a worthy endeavor—it taps us into our best self.

Part II

Amplifying Your Abilities

Leaning into Your Divine

I feel "a knowing" beyond this human existence. Something is at work—brilliantly so. In my life, I've found there to be evidence or bread crumbs. Divine has made itself utterly apparent to me via signs such as little white feathers.

> I feel "a knowing" beyond this human existence. Something is at work—brilliantly so.

I find that people sometimes get squeamish when speaking of God or Divine. I am not here to attempt a definition. I invite you to form your conclusions on what works for you. When I use the words, Divine, Source, Spirit, or Universe, please insert your own definition. What resonates with you? Collectively, a majority of people on the planet reach out to something beyond our physical existence with thought, prayer, or intention.

I feel a matrix of intelligence at work in our favor—with magical possibilities. In my life, I'm pleased to be witness to people paving a path for humanity. Healers, mediums, and somatic workers are heightening collective consciousness. Awakening souls, and practitioners are bringing their light into the world. I thank these role models who break ground for the rest of us to claim our abilities. Do you also feel high when you think of this path of expansion?

> I've shifted how I approach Source—it's now an intimate dance. I feel a sweet exchange with the abundance of the Universe.

Over time, I've developed a personal relationship with Divine rather than a removed reverence. I've felt an ever-deepening connection with Spirit. I've shifted how I approach Source—it's now an intimate dance. I feel a sweet exchange with the abundance of the Universe. The synchronicity of finding cat whiskers at key times has reinforced my path. In addition, my meditations have brought me to unfathomably colorful places. I've also felt my mediumship impressions are clearer when opening to Source. I'm able to drop into the flow of miraculous moments when my trust in Divine is deepened.

My life's journey has included an ongoing exploration of spirituality. As a child, I experienced a loving and heart-centered church. I've also chosen to leave fear-driven churches. As a young adult, I took classes from the Berkeley Psychic Institute, where I was thrilled to be among a collective group of people tuning into energetic practices. Along my quest, I attended a church where the similarities among all religions were celebrated. I've also experienced being read by psychics and mediums. Reiki practitioners, EFT professionals, and somatic bodyworkers have also had a powerful impact on my life. My spiritual journey has included life-altering messages via dreams and meditation, as well.

Have you sensed spirit moving through you? I've felt the honor to be used as a vessel to deliver messages that have ignited healing. One instance, as related, was trusting in the delivery of one single word. The word "march" meant nothing to me, but it turns out it was significant to the person receiving the gift from her departed sister. The word showed up as an incessant whispering impression at a retreat. The message didn't go away until I finally decided to share it with this particular woman. If you happen to receive messages, I recommend being sensitive to the physical setting in which you choose to share. I also recommend asking for permission when sharing. I did both in this instance.

Overall, I'm grateful to be a vessel when Spirit calls. I've taken leaps to lean into Divine and trust intuitive impressions. Another example of a random message I delivered was, "Your mom was so happy to see you in the center of the circle." Like you now, those words didn't make sense to me. But seeing a grown man cry at the significance of what those words meant to him reinforces my continued trust.

I believe we all have abilities. I also celebrate that people's abilities are of individual essence and footprint. Each of us has unique gifts that make an impact. From parenting to gardening, to coaching, our varied skills can ignite a higher world. I hope not to neglect my abilities or leave them dormant. I hope this for you too. While my skills will develop in time, I hope to expand my potential. For me, one significant step in amping my abilities is to trust in Divine and the Universe. I have learned that when I am flowing in a relationship with Source, I feel my abilities ignite. As you seek to deepen your potential, let's explore:

26. Exploration—Unanswered Hopes, Dreams, and Prayers

Have you ever had those moments when you said, "Thank goodness a particular circumstance didn't come to fruition?" Perhaps you've felt that about someone you once dated. One of the best things that happened to me was the loss of a home I was renting—a circumstance that brought me to a beautiful new town. The Universe may be offering gifts in what looks like adversity. Today might be precisely the circumstances that lead your best and brightest future. I do not recommend staying in situations that clearly scream for you to move along—such as an abusive relationship. Listen to the whisper of your innate divinity. If you have an unanswered prayer, realize that Source may be guiding you to your highest calling.

27. Exploration—A Day Communing with the Universe

Try this for an entire day. Converse—mentally share your internal thoughts with Divine—as if sharing with a good friend. What's occupying your thoughts? What's tender? What's funny? What brings elation or celebration? Interact in quiet communion. Feel your hand being held, so to speak, by the unseen force of the Universe. Pay attention to impressions or inspirations that arise. Listen with your heart. Reinforcing signs like feathers and cat whiskers show up when it feels like Divine supports impactful events in my life. Enjoy the intimate communion with the supportive forces of the Universe.

28. Exploration—Acknowledge Innate Gifts

Perhaps your most honed gifts are not mediumship or hands-on healing. You may have other signature skills to acknowledge. Maybe you're an emergency responder and can be first on the scene for unfathomable situations. Perhaps you're a teacher who creates positive ripples and alters lives forever. Maybe you are the one stranger who holds open the door, says hello, or shares a smile with a person that is teetering on edge. The possibilities are endless. Ask three of your closest friends about their impressions of your greatest talents and gifts. Let them share, and in turn, kindly acknowledge. What may seem mundane and natural to you may be of miraculous value to those receiving.

29. Exploration—Miraculous Timing

Sometimes I feel we are simply in the right time and the right place. I was once on the scene of an accident with a teen hit by a car. I was on my way to work, and as a rarity, I happened to drive a completely different direction that day for a quick errand. All in all, the boy experienced minimal injury. After EMT assessment and amongst the intense chaos of people descending on the scene to help, the boy sat alone on the curb in a dazed stupor. I felt intuitively compelled to get out of my car to sit down beside him. I almost felt witness to what came out of my mouth. With comfort, I supportively said, "For the one person who hit you, look at all of the people who showed up to help." I felt like I was supposed to be there to share this message with the boy. It felt like Divine intervention—an affirmation that I'd been guided to be at that time at that place. I'll bet some of you can recall a similar story of Divine timing. Take time to think about being on the receiving end of stories as such, as well.

30. Exploration—Follow Breadcrumbs and Feel into Open Doors

There are times when we are at the pinnacle of change—a job, a move, a big decision. A tipping point may arise, and you may not be sure which direction to head. Consider expressing your desires with Divine, let go, and then be aware of subtle (or overt) cues. Converse with your form of divinity and listen for which direction to take. If it feels it's of your highest good, it's probably your intuition speaking.

Also, be aware that stepping in the direction you feel called can sometimes come in disguise. I once signed up for a workshop because a man I was crushing on mentioned an interest in the event. To my credit, I did have a legitimate interest in the workshop. Yet my interest in this man was a specific tipping point to sign up for the event. In the end, the man had something come up, and he didn't go. Yet, because I signed up and went, my attendance introduced me to a different man who would later become a significant love of my life.

Summary

Awakening our soul awakens the world. Trusting our deepest self is trusting in miraculousness.

I am convinced our paths are supported. Nurturing an intimate relationship with Spirit heightens our intuitive guidance. Awakening our soul awakens the world. Trusting our deepest self is trusting in miraculousness.

50

Make Your Chance, Learn Your Dance
To Follow Bliss of Divine Kiss

AuthorCynthiaSingleton.com

Serendipitous Coincidences and Signs

Have you ever experienced something so miraculous that it felt beyond imaginably possible? If you tune into serendipitous coincidences, you might be astounded at the mysteries at work. This book is nothing

> If you tune into serendipitous coincidences, you might be astounded at the mysteries at work.

short of a personal miracle. One night I came home from a late-night dance class and felt overcome with the need to sit and write. Despite it being near bedtime, an idea birthed as if it were an entity of its own. I wrote the entire outline of this book until 2:00 A.M. the next morning. I felt out of touch with time and space as the book seemed to download. It's like I'd been a witness to what rolled through my fingers and onto the page.

In the coming days, I was excited about what had emerged. Yet, I hadn't taken much time to consider what direction the book might lead. And the following week—there it was.

A new publishing company was launching, and there was my direction on a silver platter! It was a solicitation for books in the same genre I'd outlined days before. I was in awe—the timing and events lined up in my favor. Without hesitation, I knew I was supposed to be a part of the new endeavor. The day after receiving the solicitation, I sent a query. With immediate response, I managed to crank out three chapters for further submission. And now here we are—an author and reader traveling this epic journey together on these pages.

Perhaps you've asked for signs or direction. Have you ever experienced a path illuminated before your eyes—where all it takes is to step into the opportunity? Are you responding to the subtle illuminations of the Universe? What if I had dismissed my chance to write this book? In the months preceding this event, I'd been stating my intention to trust the Universe. When I allowed myself to flow in Spirit's current, an opportunity synchronistically arose.

It's been amazing to discover ongoing signs. For example, I was elated when my design team for this book sent me book cover concepts. A whisker showed up the same night. It happened again the day my publishing team confirmed that I could use my kitty, Louie's face, as my book spine logo. Another whisker showed up by my computer the night I first submitted this manuscript. Writing is my passion—with the whiskers, I've felt encouraged along the way.

To this day, cat whiskers show up at significant times. At one life-altering event, I found a cat whisker under my seat. This sign foreshadowed the beautiful impact the attending people would ultimately have on my life. I found another cat whisker the night I had a first kiss with a beloved man.

Repeat numbers have been another sign. Have you experienced repeat numbers? Before I knew I would move to my beloved town of Ashland, I began noticing them. In an assigned hotel room, in a wedding invitation, and on clocks, I saw repeat numbers—often. Repetitive numbers are believed to be a sign of Divine encouragement. It turns out that this was the case for me. A short time before my move, I walked with a friend in Ashland's Lithia Park. A man dressed as a unicorn approached me there. Making no sense, he confusingly rambled about "the numbers." I kid you not. Before that day, I had been telling trusted friends about an increase in seeing repeated numbers. Then this man directly approached me to ramble about the numbers!

Coincidentally, I'd been recently telling my friends about the spiritually inclined people I'd been recently meeting. I'd been dubbing these people *unicorns*—rare and energetically inclined. Upon moving, I felt like I was in a town filled with unicorns. The unicorn-man spouting numbers in the park felt as if the Universe was reinforcing that I was on the right path. For me, moving to this vibrant town was one of the best moves of my life.

Through recent years, I've gained trust in coincidences and signs. These serendipitous happenings feel like the Universe is mischievously working in my favor. Synchronistic patterns, like the repeat numbers, are like affirming reassurances. Upon recognizing serendipitous coincidences and signs—they seem to roll in like Spirit calling cards.

For me, feathers, whiskers, and hearts are significant signs. Losing my beloved fur child, Louie, helped me trust these messages. I believe Louie bridged me to what feels like reinforcement from across the veil. After he passed, these signs appeared in perfect timing. Often when I thought about Louie, a white feather or heart-shaped object would appear in my path.

One time I found a sizable white feather on my shoulder. I'd been resting on the floor and feeling great sadness after Louie's death. I discovered the feather resting against my left shoulder. It was precisely the place on me that Louie liked to perch.

One synchronistic event was the timing leading to Louie's death. I knew my fur child was in decline from kidney disease. Months before his death, I did a lot of talking to Spirit. I did a lot of bargaining too. I asked God to either take Louie on my upcoming birthday in November or take him on Christmas. If that happened, I pleaded with Divine—I'd be assured that there was love on the other side to greet him. It turns out that the ultimate gift in my life (Louie) was given back to Divine at a significant time. I had not known that my partner at the time had also been bargaining. We discovered later that he had been pleading not to let Louie die on Christmas. So it happened an hour after Christmas. I knew with my entire being that Divine received my baby boy and dearest treasure.

The days after Louie's death were emotionally excruciating. I'd slipped into situational depression, and I grappled with how to move forward. I could not wrap my brain around life without my fur child. I felt when each new day ended; I was one step successfully closer to my own passing. I couldn't wait for the day when I'd reunite with my cherished cat. Valentine's Day approached amid my darkest days, and something quite extraordinary happened. Louie's kitty sitters, who I considered "Louie's other parents," showed up. They brought a remarkable gift. They'd commissioned a professional artist to create Louie's portrait. These friends had not known I'd been spotting hearts since Louie's death. Yet, serendipitously, when the beautiful chalk portrait arrived, the artist had drawn a small heart in the bottom right-hand corner. On top of it, she'd signed Louie's name. No one knew I'd been attributing hearts as signs of Louie. Later, I reached out to thank the artist. Unsolicited, the artist said that she felt like Louie was guiding her when creating the masterpiece. As a follow-up, I explored the artist's website. I didn't see any other portraits with a heart as Louie's had. This sign is what boosted me out of the severity of my situational depression. I knew Louie was magically working through the Universe to send me a reassuring sign of love.

Historically, Thanksgiving had been a momentous day for both Louie and me. I'd feed him an entire dish full of a variety of cat foods, meats, fruits, and vegetables (yes, he had a unique palate for food). The first Thanksgiving without him was searingly painful. In my grief, I walked outside to take in a crisp breath of fresh air. Louie loved walking outdoors in the fall to chase the autumn leaves. To my captivated surprise on that Thanksgiving morning, I discovered about *fifty* small white wispy feathers in my backyard. My grief shifted into elation. White feathers were one of Louie's signature calling cards! Miraculously, I discovered them under Louie's favorite tree. It was a place he liked to lounge in the sun—and pounce on leaves.

Another significant sign arrived when I was walking in my neighborhood. I came to a place where I often found white feathers. On this day, however, I found a fresh-cut flower directly in my path. It was white and purple—and reminded me specifically of the single flower that I'd placed on Louie's fresh grave. After finding the flower, I took a picture of it. To my amazement, the image showed a brilliant anomaly. Tremendous blinding white light surrounded the flower in the image. Many years later, this is the wallpaper picture I still use on my phone.

Before he died, I dreamt that Louie was in a bird's body, flapping above me. To this day, flapping birds and humming-birds will hover nearby at poignant times in my life. It has been years since Louie has passed, and I still receive signs. Common signs for people include butterflies, feathers, coins, and dragonflies. Can you relate to any other signs?

Electronic anomalies can also be signs. The week of starting this chapter, my dance community had an event on October 31st. In honor of loved ones, the theme was to recognize the thin veil between realms. I brought a canvas photograph of Louie and his book, *Cat Whispers*, for our community altar. When stepping into my car after the dance, the first words I heard on the airwaves had me in awe. A song's lyrics said, "I am yours, and you are mine." That was precisely the phrase that I would happily exclaim to Louie when he was alive! The same night, I had left songs playing at home for my kitty Sunshine. When I walked in my front door, a significant piece of music was playing. I broke into joyful tears when that same song unexpectedly played again. My device was not programmed to repeat songs that night. It resumed playing the other songs after that song had played twice. The lyrics to this Louie song by Meredith Andrews said, "You're not alone, for I am here."

Louie was a catalyst and continues to be a bridge to tuning into Divine. I do not doubt life beyond death. I validate that you may have experienced such tender lessons, as well, and I understand your loss. Were it not for Louie's death; I might not be writing this book today.

Enjoy comfort in the following activities:

31. Exploration—Synchronistic Coincidences

Minutes before writing this chapter, my phone randomly popped open to my digital notes page regarding signs—several times. Coincidence? To raise your intuitive awareness, pay attention to the timing of such events.

For example, when I began writing notes about pendulum work for this book, a friend of mine coincidentally brought a pendulum to my home to experiment. No one had ever done that. The same week, my mom contacted my sister and me about discovering our grandfather's military dog tag. She wondered if it was reinforcing a colossal family decision she'd made that day. On the phone call, my sister and I, without knowing the other did—pulled out a pendulum. We both got the same answer of confirmation for our mom. Take time to journal about the extraordinary coincidences you have experienced. Ask friends about their experiences too.

32. Exploration—Signs

When I initially met a significant man in my life, he had two sweet white feathers resting on his shoulder. He and I experienced an immediate

> If you would like guidance or reassurance, ask for a sign.

orbit-like bond. The Divine calling cards (feathers) were foreshadowing an incredible connection. If you would like guidance or reassurance, ask for a sign. You can also ask someone who's passed to send you a message.

I recommend doing so in the high vibration of love. Be open. Then give it time, observe, and trust!

33. Exploration—Miraculous Coincidences

Take a moment to consider the following true stories about synchronistic events:

- I have a friend who had a near death experience in a vehicle accident in New Zealand. Technically, he died. Miraculously, though, an emergency crew happened to be following his vehicle at the time. This emergency crew scrambled to restart his heart. He lived!
- I was once in a near-miss accident with a truck that rolled across the median on a snowy day. Luckily, an emergency vehicle was behind my car. Therefore, help was immediately on the scene.
- I've taken CPR courses where instructors have stated there seems to be a high instance of qualified CPR rescue officials who "happen" to be on the scene when an emergency occurs.
- I was once on a flight when a man had a heart attack. My boyfriend at the time, also on the plane—happened to be a firefighter and Emergency Medical Technician. While our aircraft landed with priority clearance, my "hero" was able to assist the man in need.

Think back to a time when you may have experienced such a coincidence. Feel free to write or reflect. Now expand this activity by asking your friends if they can recall amazing synchronicities. I suspect that this could be a more common phenomenon than most realize.

34. Exploration—Angels, Beings, or Visitations

In many of the world's religions, history depicts angelic beings in art, culture, and books. Various accounts have convinced me of the existence of these caretaking beings. An acquaintance of mine was once in an accident on a desolate bend on a country road. An unknown woman came to her driver's side window and held her hand until emergency crews arrived. When my friend inquired about this woman, no one on-scene had seen this supportive soul.

I, too, had a visitation when I was once in a serious accident. I was feeling panic while lying strapped to a backboard in an emergency room. Feeling tremendous nausea, I was fearful I would choke and die. A woman in old fashioned scrubs came to my side and looked me deep in the eyes. She cradled my hand as I sensed the energy of the Universe in her eyes. I remember calmly cooing, "You're an angel." Her hands were ice cold, but I felt such warmth. Then she said, "They will take good care of you." Note that she said, "They," despite being dressed in scrubs. After some days of recovery, I asked my partner about the angelic-like woman who calmed me in my moment of panic. I told him how she'd appeared attired differently than the other medical professionals. I shared with him how significant that moment was to me. Though my partner had been in the tiny emergency room space with me the whole time, he never saw the woman I described. Ask people if they've ever experienced something miraculous. I'm guessing some answers might be about angels, supportive beings of light, or visitations.

To further expand intuitive awareness, enjoy the depth of reading into the following summary statement a few times, slowly:

Summary

Like the symbols used to write these words—there is a deeper meaning to what I see on this page. And like my body, I'm so much more than this vessel!

Like the symbols used to write these words— there is a deeper meaning to what I see on this page. And like my body, I'm so much more than this vessel!

Intentional Vibration

In life, I often ask, "How do you live it?" Me? I hope to
shine my best light and celebrate human potential (I'm a
teacher, after all). You? How do you wish to amplify the
intuitive potential in you?

As we all well know, life offers a spectrum of highs and lows.
I've come to know that in any given circumstance, I can
choose to *act* or *react*. Have you ever felt on that razor's edge of
this decision? Even in the depths of anger and fear, I've found
that all experiences can be impacted by intention. In any
given moment, I hope to remember to *act* with compassion,
love, and empathy.

As related, a beloved friend of mine died the year I began
writing this book. He was a poster child for living fully. His
death was sudden and unexpected. Naturally, I felt absolute
sadness and anger. I let myself drop entirely into the process
of honoring the sorrow and anger. I sobbed on the floor, cried
in the car, and let the tears tenderly flow. I could not fathom
a world without his incarnate life force at play!

I embraced my grief with self-empathy and compassion. In doing so, I lifted my vibration. My intuitive senses sharpened. An extraordinary mediumship encounter happened the day after my friend's death—with absolute clarity. It's when I chose to channel my sadness into loving action.

The day after I received the news of my friend's death, I hiked to a mountaintop. It was his kind of activity. Coincidently (or not), I happened to have a beautiful stone in my daypack. I'd placed it in my pack days before, trusting that there'd be a reason for it to be there. Synchronistically, this rock was to be a natural memorial to my friend. As I stood on the mountaintop, I could see a view of Mount Shasta in the distance. It was his hometown playground. To my astounding surprise, when I pulled the rock out of my daypack, it had the exact contours of Mount Shasta. Holding the stone out in front of me, perspective wise, it was the same size and shape of Mount Shasta. The coincidence was profound.

In this raised state of loving intention, I mentally spoke to my friend. Granted, I'd had brief mediumship messages in my life, but what happened next was amazing. I experienced a full-on conversation with him. When I asked a question, he would answer. He gave me messages about his life and his death. He was telling me what he wanted his loved ones to know. My experience on that mountain top was a tremendous intuitive gift. The high vibration with which I chose to *act* after my friend's death prompted the connection.

After my hike on the mountain, I amalgamated my friend's messages into poetry form. Divinely, I was invited to speak at his memorial. I was able to read this poem to his friends and family. His ceremony took place on Mount Shasta. Though only a couple of people knew of my mediumship experience,

I read the poem to around 400 members of his beloved community. Mount Shasta held a meaningful pink alpenglow that night. I felt honored to be a vessel to transcribe his messages of love.

Life is not always easy. In our most trying times, I recommend *feeling*—which leads to *healing*. We can honor all emotions and experiences while being in raised states of vibration. I channeled my grief and sadness with loving action that still welcomed my feelings. Beautiful results transpired. The following are tools to support a raised state:

> We can honor all emotions and experiences while being in raised states of vibration.

35. Exploration—Thought Interruption

In neuroscience, it's said that "Neurons that fire together, wire together." That is, we actively build our brain cells according to the thoughts we repeat in our minds. So, if repeating thoughts of negativity, guess what your brain wires. Have you ever felt fear when reliving a moment that is no longer happening? We can interrupt unproductive thoughts and replace them with something else. When you feel the temptation of negative looping thoughts—interrupt them. Say something different to yourself. What you think creates a cascade of bodily reactions? It reinforces how we respond. How about saying something that supports you and your needs? I practiced doing this after the breakup of a catalyzing relationship. Upon feeling, processing, and grieving, I began to replace my repeated victimhood thoughts with, "I trust the Universe. Life is beautiful." My reality shifted—bringing peace.

36. Exploration—State of Being

How do you show up in the world? What state of being do you choose? You have a choice. Easier said than done, one might say. Try walking through an average day in an emotional state of tranquility. Imagine being in a world where all is Divinely orchestrated for your best and highest good. Be in each moment with an acceptance of all that shows up. Even grief. Remember that feeling grief is an indicator that we've had the honor to care genuinely. Welcome joy and invite laughter. Breathe. As if listening to your thoughts like a sporting event commentator—quiet the repeated thought patterns that are not constructive to your game. By doing so, you are practicing to calibrate your state of being.

37. Exploration—Tools of Illumination

Inspire a lifted vibration. Set the mood of a space with lighting that produces a feeling of tranquility. For me, white candles feel Divine. You could also raise your spirits by viewing a beautiful landscape by taking in nature's details. A walk on the beach lights my soul. Consider music, setting, and scenery—what lifts you? Sunsets? The night sky? Tuning in to the beauty of something outside of yourself inspires and illuminates your energetic wellness.

38. Exploration—Reframing Your Story

Recall a significantly challenging life circumstance. Now consider your story in regards to that circumstance—are you telling yourself you are a victim? What if you shifted that perspective into being a survivor? I imagine you learned great lessons about your resilience. To take it further—how about reframing your experience from being a survivor to a "thriver?"

66

Try being your own advocate with tenacious self-kindness. How you frame your experiences impacts your vibrational reality.

39. Exploration—Smudging

I've felt the vibration of a space raised by smudging. To smudge, people often use palo santo, sweet grass, or sage. Smudging is usually performed with a heat resistant dish, or shell, beneath to catch debris. The idea is to light the smudge to create a gentle drifting haze that's dispersed throughout a space. Large feathers are often used to waft the smudge. Sacred smudging is believed to purify and welcome positive energy. When I smudge, I repeat words of intention like, "I fill this space with Divine love and light." Choose what works for you. I generally accompany my smudging with invoking a feeling of reverent joy.

After purchasing sacred objects, I've smudged them before bringing them into my home. If choosing to smudge—be sure to manage optimal ventilation and fire safety. Choice items I often smudge are crystals, journals, and books.

40. Exploration—Sprinkle Energy

Have you noticed being in a space that feels stale or dense? To clear it or energetically heighten the vibration, imagine sprinkling fairy dust. I use my hands to do this as I walk through a location. You can spread positive energy in a way that feels right to you—overhand, in gentle swirls, or a mix of motions. You can also picture it like swishing water through a room. Try amping it with the intention of playfulness. Follow your intuition. I've known Reiki practitioners to walk through spaces and energetically shift a place with Reiki attuned energy. I utilize this option often, especially when traveling. Sometimes I concoct a cocktail of both Reiki and energetic fairy dust.

41. Exploration—Home Bubble

I consider my home my sacred retreat. As someone with a history of experiencing spirit visitations growing up—particularly upon waking at night, I've developed a consciousness about my space. I wrap my home in high vibrational light. I've found that asking Divine to aid in producing a powerful positive energy field helps. The key is to set an intention—mine is love and light. When I first practiced creating a white bubble around my home, I frequently visualized it. Now it is automatic that I don't often consciously think about it. Setting our vibrational intention can have an impact on the spaces we inhabit.

Summary

Elevating our energetic field elevates our intuitive capacity. Care to thrive?

Offering self-compassion at the death of my friend welcomed a clear channel for communication. Love and gratitude were the frequency. Life can be messy and chaotic. Feel to heal—and know that your energy reserves are amplified when lifting your light. Elevating our energetic field elevates our intuitive capacity. Care to thrive?

Your Energetic Field

Have you ever thought about how you are the one constant in your life? Life will swirl, and relationships will come and go. All the while, *you* are the one who will accompany your life's journey. Some might even say that you are your most significant soul mate! Do you nurture yourself as such?

What do you do to care for your energetic body—your energy field? Years ago, my life-altering slip on ice severely depleted my energy levels. When I got to the point where I could hardly walk around the block, I abandoned my full confidence in western medicine. A close friend of mine had suggested an alternative doctor for some time. Exasperated, I finally submitted to the idea of trying a whole new approach. As it turns out, it was a naturopath that ultimately impacted my recovery. This doctor not only addressed my physical being, but he offered energetic suggestions, as well. Here's an array of approaches to boost the wellness of our energy body:

42. Exploration—Mineral Baths

There are plenty of physical benefits to taking a mineral bath or immersing oneself in an Epsom salt soak. I appreciate the bliss of a healing bath, especially for muscle-tension relief, which also enhances our energetic body. I have friends who frequent natural springs on their travel destinations. The mineral waters relax the body and ease the mind. Mineral waters not only surround your physical body but also cleanse and recharge your energy field. Salt has a history of being used for ritual and protective purposes, so why not treat your energetic body to a healing soak? Epsom salts are easily accessible in general stores. Use as directed to enjoy in your own home.

43. Exploration—Walk Barefoot on Grass or a Beach

Find a place to remove your shoes and feel the wisps of grass beneath your feet. Imagine the earth soaking up tensions. Visualize the ground transmuting any stagnation—let it offer nourishment to your energetic wellness. Release and recharge. A powerful alternative is to walk barefoot on a beach. I feel intoxicated when simply imagining beach walking.

44. Exploration—Lean on a Tree

I was once a facilitator at a weekend workshop, where the organization decided to test out a new event location. The trial location turned out to be at an old mining camp. We discovered that staff and several participants at this particular camp were experiencing intense dreams. People also experienced unsettling ghostly visitations. As an energetically sensitive being, this was challenging for me. With a history of caretaking groups as an elementary school teacher, quite a bit of my energy was distracted. My reserves were depleting out of concern for our group. It happened that we also had a shamanistic woman on staff who offered a couple of good reminders for energetic wellness. She recommended I bring in my energy. Via visualization, I pictured pulling in my energy field near my body. Secondly, she suggested I lean into a tree. It was a sound reminder and grounding piece of advice. While extending gratitude against a solid tree, I closed my eyes and released my cares and worries. It was profound to discover that the comfort I felt from the tree was like the comfort of a lover spooning me in my sleep. My worries subsided in the exceptional support I found in leaning into nature's soothing pillar of strength.

45. Exploration—Elevator of Energy

An excellent way to refresh your energy field is to imagine a shaft of healing white energy. See it come up from below your feet or descending from above your head. With the speed of an elevator, let the energy flow through you as it rises or falls around your body. Imagine healing, potent energy. Let it cleanse your energetic field and immerse you entirely with restored freshness. Now picture an imaginary dial with a scale from one to ten in your head. Do an additional "elevator of energy" pass that recharges your imaginary dial to the top of the scale.

46. Exploration—Releasing into Natural Bodies of Water

My parents were once in a head-on collision with a drunk driver. Luckily the damage they faced was minor. The drunk driver was not as fortunate. My mom shared that a big part of her recovery was when she traveled to Hawaii in the following months. She immersed herself in the shoreline swells and sent out the intention of "releasing it all" into the ocean. You can try the same in other bodies of water, such as lakes and rivers. Release energy and nourish newness into your being.

47. Exploration—Giving and Service

Consider being of service. If you have kids, you are well-seasoned! Look for a simple act outside of your daily norm. Once, after a heartbreaking breakup, I picked up a broom and swept common outdoor spaces in the apartments I lived in at the time. At first, every part of my energetic being ached. Afterward, I felt lighter for stepping outside of my tender cocoon. It felt good to spread my wings for the benefit of others. A simple and ever so slight act can shift your energy.

Summary

> The energy we carry with us on our soul's journey is sacred.

> Nourish the energy that nourishes you!

The energy we carry with us on our soul's journey is sacred. Energetic loving-care boosts the soul. A mineral soak and white light imagery are powerfully healing tools. Being of service can shift stagnant or dense energy. Nature offers an abundant cleanse of the spirit. Nourish the energy that nourishes you!

Simple Meditations

What were your first intentional meditative experiences? I remember the first time I was exposed to the word "meditation." I was on the back steps of my grandparent's home. Near the dappled light of a towering avocado tree, my grandmother introduced me to the practice. I was close to kindergarten age at the time, and I still remember how relaxing and easy she made it sound. She gave me two examples of meditation. One way was to close my eyes and peacefully clear my thoughts. Another was to focus on the details of a candle flame.

At the time, everything at my age was new. Why would meditation be any different than an attempt at mastering all of the other things I was already learning? My grandmother encouraged me to try. So there I was, a five year old, staring at a candle on the concrete steps to my grandparent's backyard. I always felt my grandmother was ahead of her time. As kudos to her, she used to make veggie lasagnas, culture her yogurt, and partake in creative writing projects. Along with gifting subscriptions to fascinating magazines throughout the years, she played a significant role in my expansion.

Along with relaxing health benefits, I've come to know meditation as a way of connecting to my deepest self and Divine.

Along with relaxing health benefits, I've come to know meditation as a way of connecting to my deepest self and Divine. It is in meditation where I find that inspired ideas flutter into my consciousness. Inspiration comes when the brain's chatter calms. For me, poetry and writing ideas have budded in the emptiness. Feeling into these moments invites my intuition to blossom.

Here is a gamut of ideas for simple meditations. If distracting thoughts or feelings arise when meditating, acknowledge those passing thoughts, then place them in an imaginary vessel to revisit later if you'd like. Feel free to follow up with notes or in a journal. Enjoy choosing any of the following opportunities when you'd like a meditative reprieve. Two minutes or two hours—tailor your time as desired.

48. Exploration—Multiple Meditation Ideas

- Close your eyes and immerse yourself in relaxation and emptiness
- Focus on the details and depth of a candle flame
- Intentionally relax each part of your body from head to foot
- Create elaborate specifics of a happy place in your mind
- Watch the flowing waters of a river, creek, or stream
- Feel ocean waves as you observe them
- Fixate on a miraculous detail in nature
- Watch leaves blow on the breeze
- Listen to all the nuances of an instrumental piece of music
- Focus solely on the sensory experience of eating a piece of fruit
- Take in the details of the sky—clouds, moon, and stars
- Dip your hand in still water and then observe the droplets on your skin
- Gently stroke a flower sprig on your hands, arms, or feet
- Put a pen or paintbrush to paper and allow images to form themselves
- Focus on each of your senses, one at a time, while walking in nature
- Give full attention to musical vibration while playing an instrument
- Focus solely on your heartbeat while taking a bath
- Visit http://www.authorcynthiasingleton.com for access to guided meditations

Summary

Profound awakenings may happen in the stillness of meditation. Drop into feeling calm, relaxed, and focused. Enjoy the benefits of increased awareness, enhanced

> Profound awakenings may happen in the stillness of meditation.

health, and deepening consciousness. Meditations can be simple and easy—even for a curious kindergartener!

Dreams and Premonitions

Have you ever been astounded by particular dreams? In my younger years, I worked in a children's center. I dreamt one of the student's parents was holding a picture frame around herself. It was a dream that stayed with me. Upon arriving at work that day, the parent came into the center and held up a picture of herself in the newspaper. There it was! She was holding up her image—framed.

Dreams may reveal answers and may even be precognitive. When I lived in the Bay Area at the time of the Gulf War, I'd had another experience. It was a time of social upheaval. People were polarized about the war. So when I dreamt about ships coming home from after the war in jubilant excitement, I felt great peace. I knew our troops would be coming home soon. And they did!

> Dreams may reveal answers and may even be precognitive.

Have you ever had dreams reveal answers to you? How about precognitions? Perhaps dreams helped you resolve something. I used to have recurring dreams about an ocean liner. The dreams would come in multiple variations—embarking, being on deck, and meandering people donned in the time's clothing. I would also dream about harrowing scenes of the ship sinking. In other dreams, I'd dive below the ocean to visit a friend who had perished. My recurring dreams came to a halt when I wrote my 2012 book, *Titanic: A Tribute to the Human Spirit*. In poetry form, the writing flowed out of me the year of Titanic's 100th anniversary. Were my dreams intuitively resolving past life trauma? In writing this tribute, those recurring dreams ceased.

Dreams can provide insight and shift our experiences. To me, some feel like gifts from Spirit. I used to have recurring dreams of collecting seashells on the beach. The dreams felt euphoric and joyful. After a significant breakup, my parents invited me to travel to Florida. It was the holiday season, and I was feeling sad. A Christmas Eve storm reflected my blustery mood.

> Dreams can provide insight and shift our experiences.

On Christmas morning, we explored a small island on the Gulf Coast. My seashell dreams came true. Because of the storm, an abundance of beautiful shells had washed up on the shores. Feeling unlucky in love, I felt a sense of hope when a man approached me on the beach and gifted me with a handful of exquisite shells. It was coincidentally uplifting since the name of the island was Lover's Key. Not only had the dreams been a premonition, but the whole experience felt like a gift. I felt reminded to have hope. I trust that Divine is always sublimely at work in the highs and lows. Even in our dreams.

Dreams may also connect us with departed loved ones. Have you experienced this? After my kitty cat, Louie, had died, I had a meaningful dream encounter. I saw a sweet scene of my fur child trotting next to me in a specific location in my backyard. The dream felt enchanting and full of love! The following morning I stepped outside to the spot of the dream. I was eager to tell my then partner about the ecstatic experience. To our surprise, we found a single tuft of violets growing in the dream's exact location. Violets had never previously sprung up there in the yard! It was incredibly comforting when I later found out that violets can be a sign of connecting to heavenly realms.

I imagine some of these accounts have sparked your dream memories. Enjoy dropping deeper into your dreams:

49. Exploration—Record Significant Dreams

Record your significant dreams. In doing so, insights may dawn on you. It's been years since my Florida experience. Now is the first time I put together the serendipitous connection between Lover's Key's name and the kind stranger who extended his hand to me—a new love would come. Writing about that event in this book gave me further intuitive insight into that experience.

A pattern of dreams can indicate something meaningful. For example, I've learned that a pattern of nightmares often signifies, for me, that change is to come. Knowing this helps me let go of the dream anxiety and then relax into inevitable change coming my way.

50. Exploration—Intentional Dreaming

Before bed, set an intention about what you'd like to dream. Or try asking a question about something you've been contemplating. Your dreams may respond to your intentions and inquiries. I did this once when involved in a toxic relationship. I dreamt this man was a shooter on a school playground. In the dream, I dodged to protect myself and the children. When waking, I had the epiphany that my sacred innocence was under fire. Insightfully, that was a short-lived relationship. It reinforced a decision to stay away from this man. Setting my slumber's intention produced compelling results!

51. Exploration—Lucid Dreaming

When you're asleep, and you realize you are dreaming—play! The first thing I do when this happens is set out to the sky. I love my flying dreams. Some are like swimming breaststroke. In others, I fly to great heights—like a superhero!

Summary

Dreams are a gateway to intuition—they inspire meaning and insight. Guidance, via dreams, may arise in challenging situations. Lucid dreams invite the opportunity to play in our sleep creatively. Precognitive dreams reinforce a sense of awe —like seeing into the matrix of the Universe! We spend plenty of our lives dreaming—why not maximize the time to explore?

Science and Consciousness

Do you think about unseen energy and the way it might be influenced? I suspect if you're reading this book, you do. The human race is uncovering realities of consciousness. Science, energy, and spirit are coming together, and I'm ecstatic about the potential.

> Science, energy, and spirit are coming together, and I'm ecstatic about the potential.

Looking back in history, I appreciate shifts in what was once universally believed. Like Galileo and Copernicus, scientists risked taking a leap that shook our belief systems as we knew them. I feel we are on the precipice of another such monumental time. Since Einstein's time, scientists have been increasingly questioning the behavior of matter and energy. The basics of particles in space are under investigation at atomic and subatomic levels. Findings have concluded that particles within the space of the Universe behave in intriguing ways.

I am continually captivated by quantum mechanics, neuroscience, and such areas of scientific discovery. It feeds my intrigue regarding the connection between energy and

> I am continually captivated by quantum mechanics, neuroscience, and such areas of scientific discovery. It feeds my intrigue regarding the connection between energy and consciousness.

consciousness. How about you? We are witnessing a time of expansion, compelling research, and evidence. And this shift continues to progress—bringing increased credence to unknown phenomena.

Have you experienced the phenomenon of thinking of someone, and within minutes, they text you? Have you ever had an overwhelming feeling to check on your child or a pet, only later to realize it was wise to do so? Have you sensed a lover thinking about you from a distance?

As related to energy, I've heard intuitive mediums state that their skills show up when they get out of their thoughts. They move from the constructs of rational thought and into the depths of their intuition. People with astounding abilities have said that they often feel witness to the information that comes through from deceased loved ones.

So how does this relate to science and consciousness? Our scientifically framed understanding of energy and matter is shifting. Dr. Joe Dispenza's neuroscience and quantum physics-related explorations study such realms. I've appreciated the concept of where we direct our thoughts (energies) shapes how our brains are wired. Our brains further develop to respond to where our attention is fixed. With this, I hope to remember to be conscious of where I gaze my attention.

I feel giddy that science and spirit have become less delineated as once believed. In my lifetime alone, the word "occult" has dropped much stigma. People are

openly talking about ghosts, spirits, energy, and consciousness.
Yummy subjects! Yes? And yet,
there will always be skeptics and
critics. Every day was not a walk
in the park for history's shakers of

> I feel giddy that science and spirit have become less delineated as once believed.

truth. Granted, with some audiences, I choose my conversations carefully. Skeptics may be slow to develop their ideas
about intuitive consciousness. One only needs to be open to
exploration and discovery.

Let's consider science and consciousness:

52. Exploration—Energy Experiment

Quantum physicists have observed particle interactions
in the space that makes up the Universe. Our world
is vastly energetic. We are not mere flesh and body
systems. We are more. To tune into your energetic
field, rub your hands together. Then hold your palms
up, face to face, and slowly bring them toward one
another. Vacillate/bounce the movement of your
palms, ever so slightly, without ultimately touching
them together. Play to see if you can sense energy
sensations between your palms.

53. Exploration—Multidimensional Places

In quantum mechanics, studied particles have been
discovered to be in two places at once. That is, one
particle can exist in two places at the same time. If
particles can be in two locations simultaneously, what
can we inquisitively explore when it comes to our human
capacity? Can our own energy be in multidimensional
places? For further insight into this concept, consider
the possibility of what it might be like to be in two places
at once. Imagine where you'd want to be if you *could* be

in two locations. Picture everything in great detail—sights, sounds, tastes, smells, feelings.

54. Exploration—Entanglement Impact

I find quantum entanglement intriguing. Once separate particles have been introduced, they are forever entangled, even at great distances. Does this encourage the idea that thoughts and emotions can be shared over great distances? To illustrate this concept, try thinking intently of a loved one you've not heard from in a while. Choose someone you enjoy exchanging conversation with but haven't spoken with in a bit. Think intently of that person for a few days in a row. You might ignite an energetic connection and hear from that person in the not too distant future!

55. Exploration—Intentional Transformation

In quantum studies, it was revealed that an observer's intention could impact particles' behaviors. Play with this concept to understand it further. To do so, choose a meaningful word such as love, gratitude, or tranquility. Influence your surroundings by putting it out in the Universe—practice saying that word, with meaning, at least three various times in a day. Give it a week and evaluate the results of your intention. For example, you might notice more love in your life when focusing on the word *love*. Moving forward, try other intentional words and see if they impact your surroundings.

Summary

When it comes to science and consciousness, we're witness to a scientific tipping point in history. Particles in the space we inhabit have been found to:

- Be impacted without touch
- Become entangled at great distances
- Be influenced by intention

These findings inspire me to consider the energy around my body and the impact I can bring into my life with intention. As Dr. Joe Dispenza said in this chapter's initial quote, "The quantum field responds not to what we want; it responds to who we are being."

Electronic Phenomenon

If we want to find the secrets of the universe, think in terms of energy, frequency, and vibration.
—Nikola Tesla

Speaking of the human impact on energy, I think of another fascinating phenomenon. Have you seen electronics act oddly around you or someone else? I happen to have a cherished friend who has a history of influencing electronics. He participated in Psychic Studies classes at UC Santa Barbara years ago. In a laboratory setting, he could shift the results of a random number generator to results that were not so random. This conclusion is but one testament to human influence on electronics.

Have you heard about particular people having difficulty wearing watches because the batteries die quickly? Are you such a person? A theory is that the person's energetic field influences the batteries.

A friend of mine once set off an unplugged carbon monoxide detector when merely holding it in her hand. It had been sitting for years without batteries. While these experiences are not so easily explained, it's a genuine phenomenon. Have you witnessed (or experienced) unexplained incidents as such?

The same people generally experience street lights popping on or off in their passing presence. There's something to be said about this lamppost phenomenon when it happens rarely. Yet, for some people, it's a common occurrence. A variety of electronic events often occur around these people.

As related, I knew someone to power on an unplugged TV. She worked in a children's center and was encouraging young stragglers out of a classroom. Kids outside needed supervision, so she was eager for them to move along. She was using swooping gestures while giving directions. The TV was in the path of this teacher and the doorway to the playground. To her energy and arm gestures—whoosh, the TV flashed on into a state of static. The surprising anomaly prompted the teacher to inspect the safety of the situation. In checking the TV's power cord, she discovered the TV was unplugged.

I once witnessed an empty car start in the presence of a person who had a history of impacting electronics. The vehicle did not have the capability to remote-start. This person was feet away from the car when the motor turned. She was leaving a joyous and soulful event and was in a hurry to make it across town to a favorite class. Time was tight, and her energy was high as she eagerly approached the vehicle. The car engine did not only start from a distance. When opening the car door, the dials on the dashboard darted back and forth wildly.

> Some suggest those who experience electronic phenomenon have big vibrational energy fields.

It's a common theory that people who influence electronics are highly vibrational, positive people. Some suggest those who experience electronic phenomenon have big vibrational energy fields. Some suggest influential beings from other realms, such as guides or angels, impact a person's surrounding energy.

And then, there are other unexplained electronic phenomena. Has a significant song played on the radio at a critical moment after a loved one passed? Have you experienced a song that seems to "show up" when needed most? Or how about a playlist playing a meaningful song out of order on an electronic device?

Have you experienced the phenomenon of cell phones acting funny in certain situations? At synchronistic times? One comical account of such an event is when a friend told me of a time she was about to be intimate with her partner. Her cell phone's voice-assist warned from the nightstand, "That's okay! As long as you don't do anything dangerous." There was another time when a dear friend and I had just finished facilitating a weekend workshop. We were in an unusually elevated state of vibration. And we were so tired; everything seemed hilarious. While hysterically laughing together, her untouched phone's voice assist randomly chimed in with, "LOL!"

The day after I began writing this chapter on electronic phenomenon, I happened to be at a dance event where an electronic phenomenon encounter was shared. The woman sharing had no idea I was writing this book. As a facilitator, she'd put together a music playlist for the dance event. She said that, despite efforts at home, she couldn't delete the long pauses between songs. However, she reported that when she played the songs for our event, the silences were no longer there. The playlist timing had magically remedied itself the day of the dance. It was not until after the dance, in a group circle, did she share this experience. A tangible phenomenon occurred involving the electronic spaces between songs.

You might enjoy some discoveries while trying the electronic phenomenon exercises below:

56. Exploration—Flashlight Energetics

Try holding a flashlight in your hands and concentrate on it with the light switch in the on position. For your comfort, no need to look directly into the light. Focus solely on the intention of turning off the light without touching the switch. When approaching this task, empty your thoughts and calm your mind. The only thought you might try is the word "off," directed into the flashlight's entirety. Do so with patience, relaxation, and love. If one flashlight doesn't work, try others. Whether you create results or not, you've given it a try. This exercise provides further understanding of how electronic phenomenon might be tapped into with intentional practice. If you produce results, enjoy recording them on video, showing that the on/off button on the flashlight remained untouched.

57. Exploration—Nightlight Focusing

I've known a person to look at a nightlight and dim it into darkness by intention. When the person stopped their focus on dimming the light, it returned to its natural illumination. The person claims to have done this by releasing all thoughts. They said they funneled all of their energy, intending to dim the light. Their state of mind was in a calm and positive meditative state of focus. It was as if absolutely no other thoughts of anything else existed. Everything was 100% focused on the light.

To try, go into a room free of any other lights. Be still with quiet confidence. Funnel all of your intention and energy into a nightlight. Do so as if you and it are the only things that exist on this planet. Intend the nightlight to dim. Feel free to try doing so with emitting intention from your hands, as well. Let go of wanting it so bad that it could interrupt the meditative benefit of the task. Be Zen. Results, or not, you have experience on the subject of electronic phenomenon.

Summary

If you've lived with electronic phenomenon, you are not alone. Perhaps you have related stories. Wristwatch batteries dying, streetlights popping on and off, and cash registers acting odd are common occurrences. Some people experience electronic anomalies more than others. Enjoy these practices to ignite further awareness of this intuitive gift. While electronic phenomenon may not be fully understood, I'm confident unsuspecting people may be pleasantly surprised—perhaps you!

> If you've lived with electronic phenomenon, you are not alone.

Tips for the Empath

If you are reading this book about expanding your intuition, the chances are that you are a highly empathetic person and maybe even an empath. Do you tend to feel others' emotions? Do

> An empathetic person can relate to someone's emotions, while an empath can feel and experience the emotions as if they are their own.

you sometimes feel overwhelmed with sudden emotion in public locations with no explanation? Does it take you time to recover from group events, parties, or large gatherings? When you've been around a friend, acquaintance, or individual experiencing deep feelings, can you feel those as if your own? If you've said yes to any of these questions, you may be an empath. An empathetic person can relate to someone's emotions, while an empath can feel and experience the emotions as if they are their own.

When I was a young girl, I remember going into a favorite restaurant with my mom, who was meeting friends for lunch. Upon entering the restaurant, I felt comfortable, at ease, and excited about tasty food. Once the group arrived,

I remember beginning to feel entirely overwhelmed by unexplained sadness. I sat with it for a bit and eventually left the table to head to the bathroom to release intangible tears. I was wholly baffled. For many years, that experience left an impression on me because I could not figure out how to articulate that experience to myself or my mom. It was years later, I learned from energy workers that I am an empath. Only then did I understand that event. The baffling childhood experience that stayed with me for years finally made sense. I genuinely believe I had been experiencing someone else's emotions in that restaurant. I'd had other experiences as a child, but that particular experience held a lot of shame and embarrassment. Upon eventually realizing I was an empath, I took the opportunity to recognize and release my confusion around that experience—out of compassion for my abilities.

You may also carry shame and guilt regarding your empathic abilities, but I invite you to look at your skills as a superpower. You were born with a gift! You can feel others on a level so deeply that a person in your presence can feel wholly understood—often without words. There is a flip side to these abilities that can impact your well-being if you do not practice self-care tips. Let's explore some of those here.

Like many interested in abilities and healing awareness, you're probably an empath. The world can benefit from your gifts. With that, there are supportive ways to take care of yourself. Rather than going into hiding, one can practice self-care tips to make it easier for your empathic nature to shine in all walks of life.

I hope my once and sometimes rocky road will pave the way for your smooth journeys ahead. The following are foundational tools. One may call to you most, and all of them may be of service. Always keep in mind to consider if rising emotions are your own to process first with self-compassion. The following are supportive practices, in either case. These exercises nurture your empathetic, energetic field:

58. Exploration—Bring in Your Energetic Field

Keep in mind that your energetic field might be quite large. You may be sweeping up other people's vibrations as you go about your day. Several people see "auras" around people and other living things. If you don't see auras, you can imagine light emanating all around your body. By visualizing this energy surrounding your body being pulled closer to your skin, you can feel less permeable to outside influences. Bring in this biofield to surround your body by 15 to 20 inches as you carry out your day.

59. Exploration—Intention Proclamation of Release

Try stating the following with intention and love, "I release anything in my energy field that is not mine or of my highest good. I replenish my space with optimal health and wellness." Take a few focused breaths, with your exhale being longer than your inhale. Imagine your body and energy field immersed in loving white light.

60. Exploration—Earth Grounding and Ethereal Filling

Imagine a cord connected to the base of your spine that extends deep into the earth. Visualize releasing unnecessary energy down into the ground. After doing so, picture it sealed below your feet. Then, top off your energy with positive white light via a receiving cord through your head's crown.

61. Exploration—Bathing in Light

When taking a shower or a bath, picture the water infused with recharging white light. Imagine the water transmuting intensity and saturating you with healing and wellness. You can do the same thing in the ocean, lakes, rivers, and other water bodies.

62. Exploration—Crystal Globe Relief

When your energy is feeling congested with anxiety, picture yourself in an imaginary crystal globe. Cup your hands around this imaginary sphere and gently blow at it with love and compassionate intention. Visualize that each breath brings clarity, healing, and wellness.

Summary

Your intuitive compassion brings healing to those in your life—and the world! Practicing self-care tips supports your energetic foundation. These practices enable you to share your empathic gifts without exhausting your abilities. Your gifts are your superpower!

Your gifts are your superpower!

An Empath Is a Sacred
Feeler and Healer

AuthorCynthiaSingleton.com

Visitations

I felt smatterings of frustration when initially searching for a quote for this chapter. When using the keyword "ghost" in my online search, a plethora of information flooded my computer—much with a negative connotation. These search results triggered a childhood memory that was somewhat traumatic until I understood it in my later years. The event was when my sister and I were invited to our first slumber party as young girls. At bedtime, the small group of girls suggested we share ghost stories. My sister and I rose with great excitement, eager to tell listeners about the actual ghost that lived in our then childhood home.

My sister and I were not aware that ghosts were not a universal phenomenon for people—until we began to share our stories. She and I were lucky to live our younger years accepting unknown phenomenon without parental discouragement. When sharing our real ghost stories, we'd learned the hard way that many others had not grown up as we had. It was the dawning of understanding societal fear and rejection of ghosts. That was one of my first memories of "going into hiding" in my fascination with the unknown. I'm now happy to feel times are changing.

To clarify, as a child, I thought of all spirits as ghosts. I now consider "ghosts" as being earthbound spirits. I feel spirits have the ability to travel a multitude of realms. I do not claim to have all the answers related to ghosts and spirits. I'm sharing from my lifetime of interest and direct experiences.

If you're like me, you may occasionally experience spirits in your field. These visitations may show up in different ways—perhaps as lights, shapes, forms, sounds, smells, dreams, electronically, or via sensory impressions. That given, you may or may not want direct encounters. Maybe you've been impacted by societal stigma about ghosts and have shut yourself off from such phenomena.

Coincidentally, the night of writing this chapter, I came across a young man who worked at a local chocolate shop. He said all of his coworkers had experienced encounters. Everyone who worked in the building, he said, except for him.

For many years of my life, I'd been an avid watcher of shows investigating ghostly activity. When watching, I made efforts to filter out the glitz and special effects that stigmatized spirits as scary. The overall suggestive evidence of spirit existence was palpable. I've always appreciated the programs that would respectfully interact with souls. Investigations sometimes revealed that spirits were attempting to leave a comforting message for a beloved. As such, I particularly appreciated the show called *The Haunting Of...* with medium Kim Russo. She's offered comfort to many celebrities regarding their experiences they first thought of as terrifying. It turns out there were often explanations that were far less intimidating than first perceived.

Where do you stand when it comes to visitations? You might be well versed in the subject. Are you someone who wishes to have firsthand accounts? Let's consider ways to approach interacting with ghosts in physical locations. If you've not

> Where do you stand when it comes to visitations?

already had direct encounters, it's not out of the question that you may have a brush at some point. If this triggers fear, I encourage you to evaluate your viewpoints, especially related to societal stigma.

I believe we can have an influence and impact on our encounters. As I revisit scenes from some of the vast ghost shows I've viewed, I found something evident. When spirits were approached with great fear and anger, the experience was generally not pleasant. Energetically, those approaches fed more of the same—fear and anger. When welcomed with grounded compassionate respect, it seemed ghosts were generally cooperative.

As related, I was at an amusement park one October, where zombie-like actors wandered the premises for guests' entertainment. Interestingly enough, the ghouls seemed particularly interested in approaching the people who were reactively spooked. The characters weren't as interested in those who would respectfully acknowledge their presence. When I stayed grounded and smiled at their approach, I'd get a nod of respect. Can this then be transferred to real-world experiences? That is, fear feeding fear and respect promoting mutual respect?

The following are activities that I have found helpful in encounters.

63. Exploration—Space Boundary

Perhaps you are sensitive to spirit "traffic" in or around your home, which can be overwhelming. If you'd rather not have visitations in your space, you can create an energetic boundary. To do so, respectfully say out loud that your home is your sacred sanctuary where you'd like to be free of visiting spirits. Create a proclamation that resonates best for you. You can adjust the number of times you announce this depending on the amount of spirit activity—once a day, once a week, or once a month should suffice. Keep in mind that if you are open to receiving supportive spirit messages within that boundary, you can state that intention, as well. While proclaiming your bounds, visualize a white-light space bubble around your home.

64. Exploration—Acknowledgement and Respectful Intention

My sister and I serendipitously discovered that when we travel places, we respectfully acknowledge potential ghosts. We state an intention in hotel rooms or spaces we will be sleeping. We are both sensitive to spirits and yet appreciate a good night's sleep. My words of intent often go like this, "If there are any spirits or ghosts in the vicinity, I respect you, and thank you for sharing your space. Please do not show yourself or make yourself known unless you've come to deliver a positive message for me. Thank you, thank you."

65. Exploration—Encounter Perceptions

Keep in mind that encounters that seem malevolent may not be. They could be a catalyst to alter someone's direction. For example, someone on a self-destructive life trajectory might have an intense visitation. It might catalyze a person to make positive life changes. I once knew of a young man whose girlfriend was being impacted by a presence. It appeared that this apparition was a good reminder to the young man about how he, himself, treated his girlfriend. If you have persistent unexplained activities of concern, I recommend seeking help. Look for a reputable source such as a skilled medium with excellent references. They can help assess the situation and give specific guidance as related.

66. Exploration—Asking for a Message

Spirits may try to make contact. They can show up at your bedside. You might sense a brush on your cheek. They may repeatedly show up in dreams. To clarify the reason for their presence, ask if they have a message. Spirit communications can come in many ways, such as pictures, sounds, smells, and symbols. In these cases, we often learn that a passed loved one has a meaningful healing message.

67. Exploration—Creating Boundaries

If you happen to be an individual who already receives many messages from spirits, you can set boundaries. If a presence shows up in your space that you do not want to communicate with, you can say so. One limit might be stating that you do not wish to receive messages while you are sleeping. You can say this out loud before bed. I've also heard of intuitives "setting hours" with spirits. They tell spirits that they only have permission to make contact during a specific frame of time.

68. Exploration—Clarifying a Message

When trying to understand a message, you can solicit further clarification. You can ask for a picture or a symbol. I once heard the word "baubles" from a loved one who had passed. It made no sense, and I struggled to understand. Finally, I asked for a picture. When I saw a mental impression of "bubbles," I instantly broke into heartfelt tears. That word is significant to my family. In some of our happiest moments, we say, "This is a bubble." It acknowledges our most treasured moments in time as a "memory bubble."

69. Exploration—Calling in a Visitation

Have you ever felt a location to be haunted? I once stayed at a historic lodge where I felt spirit activity immediately upon arrival. I was with a friend who'd not experienced a spirit visitation to date. He was fascinated to explore. So we sat down and declared a loving invitation:

- We respectfully acknowledged spirit presence on the property
- We thanked the spirits for sharing space in that location
- We stated we were interested in evidence of spirit presence
- We asked kindly for the beings to provide us with tangible evidence
- We asked for only respectful messages
- We extended our gratitude for their potential gift

During that stay, my friend awoke to what felt like a hand creating gentle weight impressions actively on the bed around where he slept—multiple times. With that, he mentally asked the spirit to touch his hand as confirmation of its presence. At that, my friend felt a gentle tingle skim across his palm.

That weekend I heard a sharp scraping sound across the headboard and a loud pound on the bathroom door. This single-level end unit room was far from other guest access on the remote property. To rule out noise pollution from other sources, I was able to reproduce the same headboard and bathroom door sounds from within the confines of our room.

70. Exploration—Promote Connection with Raised Vibration

Perhaps, like me, you've lost someone in this physical world that altered your entire reality. In losing my beloved feline fur child Louie, I allowed the sadness to move through me. I also channeled much of my grief into loving endeavors in memory of Louie. One act of celebration was to have the words, "Whisper an epic tale of magnificent scale, with whiskers, fur, and feline allure," placed on his headstone. Semi-precious stones, tulips, and daffodils cheerfully mark his grave in honor of his colorful life. His book, *Cat Whispers*, was created out of devotion for our connection. As a tribute, I mailed *Cat Whispers* to an animal shelter in each of the 50 United States. Accompanied was a note of gratitude to those who make a difference in animals' lives. Despite Louie's death, our energetic connection remains strong.

I've heard several testimonials of parents who, when raising their vibration, can receive clearer messages from their deceased children. They had processed initial sadness and learned to come to terms with anger or guilt. Connection with their child was heightened when they eventually allowed themselves moments to laugh and experience the joy life offers. I've heard mediums say that our loved ones want us to live fully and celebrate memories. May my story, and theirs, inspire the concept of raising one's vibration for increased connection. Communing with your deceased loved ones and asking for signs may create an incredible new form of relationship with those who have passed. For me, my fur child's death helped bridge a deeper connection to Spirit and Divine.

Summary

Ultimately, encounters may promote insight, catalyze change, and provide powerful healing!

Our intentions can impact visitations. Do you want to connect? What boundaries might you set? Spirits may wish to be acknowledged or to offer encouragement. Ultimately, encounters may promote insight, catalyze change, and provide powerful healing!

Fear Feeds Fear
While Respect
Promotes Respect

AuthorCynthiaSingleton.com

Crossing the Veil

Altered consciousness can take us to unexplained places. Have you ever felt meditation feel as if it shifted you into other realms? For me, crossing the veil has been the epitome of merging my intuition and Divine. Meditation has been my gateway to crossing the veil.

> Meditation has been my gateway to crossing the veil.

In some of my deep meditations, I have a recurring experience. I'm transported to another place and time, as another person. In this familiar setting, I find myself standing near a primitive and slender footbridge. I am a person who stands in mindless contemplation, feeling shallow river waters flow on the edge of grassy lands. I'm wholly absorbed in the drifting sensation that cleanses my soul. When I'm this other person, my meditative time feels like a frequent ritual. I wonder if, perhaps, this was a significant past life memory. I suspect that dropping into a tranquil state of meditation can trigger a soul remembrance.

Other meditations have transformed into heightened feelings and imagery. For example, this has happened to me in *Relaxation Pose* at the tail end of yoga classes. Laying on my mat, I can slip into vivid places of light and color, into what feels like whole scenarios of different times and places. In one encounter, I was another woman in a small village. It felt as if I might be somewhere like Ireland or Scotland. I wore a celebratory white dress, and my long red hair danced on the breeze in grassy fields. Children ecstatically frolicked around, carrying ribbons that undulated on the fragrant air. More than dreamlike, it brought tears to my eyes.

And now, I choose to share my most profound meditation experience. One that changed my life forever. I've been selective as to whom I've shared this story, until now. I hope it may ignite an understanding of the capacity to travel into another realm. My account started with the most devastating heartbreak of my life—losing a most beloved soul. The fact that he had four legs and whiskers was wholly beside the point. I had not born a human child into this lifetime, and my kitty Louie Dewey Mocha Latte was my EVERYTHING. My bambino—he and I, deeply soul connected. I could go on and on about my love for Louie, which I illustrated in my book, *Cat Whispers*. Ultimately, our shared love was the catalyst that transported me across the veil.

It was not long after Louie passed that I did a guided meditation to introduce me to my spirit guides. A turn of events in this meditation took me to an astonishing "place." This experience was ground zero to catapulting me into a new life trajectory. My connection with Spirit amplified—considerably.

This guided meditation gave directions to step into a clearing to meet a being. When I did, my beloved fur child was there to greet me. He was at the top of a gazebo's steps. In reuniting with him, I held him against my left shoulder as I often did in this lifetime. I found it curious that I didn't feel his usual weight, which later made sense—I was supporting his *spirit* body against mine. I felt permeating, overwhelming love. So much so that as I write this now in remembrance, I do so with tears of gratitude. Beautiful imagery appeared around the gazebo—sunsets on tropical beaches and fragrant blowing highland grasses. I "felt" music as I subtly rocked in dance with Louie.

The experience transitioned into what I would describe as Louie's life review. We were graced with multiple flashes of moments we had shared. From playful moments as a small kitten to his tender death in my arms on one silent night, I felt the entirety of our entwined beautiful life.

Then our surroundings shifted again. A grand formation of light beings encircled us and looked upon us with admiration. There is no earthly vocabulary to describe these energetically, supportive beings. They were translucent, floating forms that visually looked like iridescent bluish-silverish liquid mercury. In witness to us, they *were* the exquisite essence of love.

In Louie's life, I would often exclaim during our happiest of times, "May God and angels watch over us." I felt an unspoken understanding that this circle of angelic beings had affirmatively witnessed Louie's and my life. Colors and vibrations in this realm were inexplicable. And the sweetness of emotion was incomprehensible.

On a side note, I did a personal piece of research to reference this experience. I had the opportunity to participate in a legal Ayahuasca journey. Ayahuasca, a ceremonial brew made from a South American vine, is known to have the capacity to take people into the spirit realm. In confirmation, the Ayahuasca took me to the same realm. Going across the veil is now like tuning into a radio dial—where I can often retrieve or receive messages.

Who might you want to connect to in the spirit realm? Would you be open to a message from across the veil? Below is a guided meditation for your exploration. Keep in mind that high vibration has promoted my travels into the spirit realm—approach these meditations with a sense of openness, reverence, and love. Find a quiet place where you can rest and close your eyes. You might ask a friend to read the prompts below, providing significant pauses between steps. You may also visit my website at http://www.authorcynthiasingleton. com for guided meditations and additional inspirations.

71. Exploration—Crossing the Veil Meditation
Remember to pause between each prompt:

- *Find a place where you can quietly rest and close your eyes*
- *Visualize yourself surrounded in Divine light*
- *Gently set the intention of "allowing"*
- *Quiet all of your senses by focusing solely on relaxation and breath*
- *Imagine being in a tranquil location of your choice, like a garden or a cabin in the woods*
- *Visualize the details in this sacred place*
- *From here, you see a door or gateway*
- *Approach it, continuing to breathe deeply*
- *Picture specific details of this door or gateway*
- *Imagine a sacred being greeting you at this passageway*
- *Enjoy a moment to welcome and acknowledge one another*
- *Follow this guide to a beautiful nature trail*
- *Travel up this magnificent path, focusing on sights, scents, and sounds*
- *Pass by a waterfall, and then river that runs alongside of your path*
- *Enjoy the wonder of this luminous place*
- *Continue to journey deeper on your path until you reach an open clearing*
- *Stop and look at the natural beauty of your surroundings*
- *In this clearing, you see a structure—like a lodge, or a gazebo*
- *Approach the structure and enter slowly*
- *Your guide will wait here, at the doorway, for your return*
- *Note that the details of this structure may change each time you're here*
- *Follow your intuition to a chosen location within this structure*
- *When you get there, a being is waiting for you there*
- *You might notice other beings, as well. You are supported here*

- *Greet one another with gratitude*
- *See if they have a message for you*
- *Take some minutes to receive the offering*
- *If you do not understand, ask to be given the message in another way*
- *Take in this message—welcome what comes with all of your senses*
- *Acknowledge this gift with love and extend your gratitude*
- *It's time to leave soon*
- *Knowing you can return here—say goodbye for now*
- *Go back to the guide who has waited for you at the entry door*
- *Retrace your steps with this guide, along the path that brought you here*
- *Return to where this journey first began today*
- *Take a moment to thank your guide and say goodbye for now*
- *Step back into where you started*
- *Come back to the location where your body is physically resting now*
- *Slowly move your toes and fingers*
- *Gently become aware of your arms and legs with small movements*
- *Take a few revitalizing breaths*
- *And slowly open your eyes*
- *Welcome back*

Now, without pause, take the time to journal or reflect upon the highlights of your experience.

Summary

Opportunity is at your doorstep—deep meditations, accompanied by loving gratitude, can take you to extraordinary realms. When elevating into altered consciousness, your intuitive capacity is maximized. Enjoy the power of where your spirit can take you!

> When elevating into altered consciousness, your intuitive capacity is maximized.

Extraordinary Realms Are Accessible via Your Own Consciousness

AuthorCynthiaSingleton.com

Past Lives

Have you heard of people claiming to have been Cleopatra or King Tutankhamun? I question how many people could claim to have been so in a past life. With that, I know a hypnotherapist who wondered if people were "in imagination" instead of remembering past lives. I think this can be true. Sometimes.

Yet, what of the accounts of past lives that can be traced to tangible details? Conceivable? A vast amount of collected testimonies support past lives. Dr. Ian Stevenson is one pioneering expert who gathered a compelling collection of past lives. He was particularly interested in children's testimonies of coinciding birthmarks related to their previous life's death. Dolores Cannon, author, and hypnotherapist developed past life regression techniques. Within her work, she did research to verify the characteristics of culture and places, as demonstrated in people's testimonies. Initially, a skeptic, Brian L. Weiss, MD, a graduate of Yale Medical School, is also a notable contributor to past life regression and therapy techniques.

> A vast amount of collected testimonies support past lives.

People have been known to accurately describe times and places they've never been in this lifetime. Some have drawn maps of streets, towns, and architecture with historical accuracy. Intricate details from historical events have been relayed in previous life testimonies. There are accounts of people tracing names of acquaintances or family members from past lives. Many people have greatly improved the quality of their life by healing traumas via past life regressions. Perhaps you have stories of your own.

Have you ever had a feeling of deja vu about a new place? The first time I visited Victoria, British Columbia, I felt deja vu—again and again. It was an all-encompassing feeling. The architecture, the streets, the bay, the energy, the smell—all felt so familiar. How is that? Walking around street corners only revealed a further sense of familiarity around each bend. To date, I've not visited anywhere else that resembles Victoria, including Europe. Yet, I feel at home in Victoria, Canada. I'm curious if I'd had a past life there. Have you felt the same way about a particular place?

Some people have recurring dreams about familiar places— only to find that they are not imaginary or fictional. How about you? I used to have dreams of walking in robes in a hot desert location. I remember the feeling of the crunch of sand beneath my sandals. In this location, there were caves, rock-built structures, and stones. I'd not recognized a place like this in my current life. In my forties, a friend invited people to view a slideshow of her visit to the Middle East. When shown, I couldn't believe what I was witnessing— and feeling. Slide after slide revealed places so familiar to my dreams that it brought tears to my eyes. No one at the gathering knew what I was experiencing. I didn't talk outwardly about such things then. After the event, though,

I told my partner about my experience. I was restless that night, in the wake of the familiar imagery.

Have you witnessed children's receptivity? There are several accounts of young children remembering past lives. Long ago, I worked in a children's center. I remember sitting at a table, drawing with preschoolers. I was astounded to see elaborate detail to a picture being made by a young boy sitting across from me. He'd drawn a western town. Each building in the image was filled with texture and detail. In the middle of the picture was a tall cowboy. The hat, clothing, holsters, and spurs caught my eye. I'd not seen a child at this age draw a picture in such detail and perspective. Open-endedly, I invited the boy to tell me about his drawing. His response was, "This was me when I lived in the olden days."

In addition to this story, a friend of mine had a fascinating experience as a young girl. Too young to remember much, her mom retells this event. The story goes that they were traveling from Oregon to the San Francisco Bay Area. While there, they visited an antique store. The two of them began looking through an old picture album. My friend recognized a woman in the album. Quite excitedly, my friend incessantly repeated the woman's name over and over to her mom. She told her mom that the woman was a neighbor. Granted, these were antique pictures. My friend went on to exclaim that the woman in the photograph "died in the fire." My friend's mom was baffled at her young child's claims—until she turned the page. Evidently, on the next page, there was an article about the woman. The article revealed the same name of the woman that my friend had exclaimed. The article also reported that the woman died in a fire.

Do you have compelling past life accounts? Maybe you know someone who has. When I was in high school, two of my best friends had separate recurring dreams of being husband and wife in a previous life. They'd been close friends since early childhood in this lifetime. I found it quite touching that the two danced a preplanned brilliant ballroom waltz together when the other got married.

Have you ever felt so closely connected to someone that you suspect you've had another life together? To date, of this book's publication, I've had only one past life regression session. I was regressed to a few lives, including a meaningful life in Egypt. I was able to recall the thin white dress I wore. I could feel the ground beneath my sandals. I was in an open-air temple with large pillars and wide terraced steps. I was a woman of social status. Multiple sisters and people surrounded this life.

As related, I wound up at an event in recent years—where I was highly intrigued by a particular man. An exercise at the event was to eye gaze with one participant at a time for a couple of minutes. The task had nothing to do with past lives. I found myself flabbergasted when I came face to face with the man who'd earlier caught my eye. He felt Divinely familiar, and I heard myself mentally saying, "It's me. It's me. It's me." In the silence, while looking into his eyes, I was surprised by my loud thoughts. For months, I'd not revealed to him what I'd experienced the night I met him.

After some time of eventually getting to know him well, I saw an opportunity to ask, "Do you think we've known each other in a past life?" I'd given him no access to any information, whatsoever, about the Egyptian life I'd recalled. He had no clues, no detail, and no hints. Being an energetically gifted man, he took a moment to go inward and reflect.

He began to describe seeing me in Egypt. He described the woman I embodied and the thin white dress I wore. He mentioned my sandals and the hard sand-like ground. He spoke of the open-air temple with giant pillars. He referred to wide terraced steps. As he described, I could see his eyes move around while he recalled the sights. He spoke of the people that surrounded my life because of my social status. He had described (exactly!) what I'd recalled in my past life regression. Again, he had no idea I'd said precisely the same things in my session years prior. The details rang true. By the time he'd shared, I was in sweet tears. I appreciated that he was able to tune into the recognition as well.

I imagine you may be thinking of instances related to past lives. Perhaps you've had recurring dreams of familiar places where you've never traveled. Maybe you have accounts of past life memories. Is there a place, to you, that rings deja-vu-true? Have you known a young child to speak of astounding past life details? Below are activities for further exploration:

72. Exploration—Familiar Souls

If you feel a previous life connection with a close friend or family member, explore together. Sit apart from one another with separate notepads. Concentrate on the concept of tuning into a shared past life. If you'd had conversations about this before, stay away from the details you already know. Feel into what you don't know. Take about ten minutes to write down thoughts or images related to a possible shared life. When done, come together to compare. Do some of your notes match or correlate?

73. Exploration—Mirror Impressions of Past Lives

In a softly lit space, without distractions, look into a mirror. In the spirit of intention for the highest good, let your eyes relax as you focus on energetically embodying past lives. Be calm, refrain from facial expressions, and let visuals come to you. Do images of a prior self superimpose over your reflection in the mirror? Follow up with notes or impressions.

74. Exploration—Past Life Partner Work

Sit across from a trusted partner, both surrounding yourself Divine light and set an intention to reveal past life clues. One person is the sitter, while the other is the reader. In a softly lit room, take about ten minutes each to softly gaze at one another. The reader looks for past life clues, while the sitter openly relaxes without movement or expression. Much like the above exercise, the reader watches to see if images of prior lives superimpose upon the sitter. Share your observations after each sitting. Perhaps you'll discover something that resonates with each of you.

Summary

> You might realize that access to past life remembrance is more common than people openly discuss.

I'm fascinated by past life accounts. Do you have related stories? May you enjoy the possibility of discovery in these explorations. You might realize that access to past life remembrance is more common than people openly discuss.

126

Past Lives—
Familiar Souls
Share Varied Roles

AuthorCynthiaSingleton.com

Near Death Experiences

ike me, have you felt a fascination around the topic of near death experiences? Bestselling author Dr. Raymond Moody, renowned for his research, has dedicated much of his life to studying NDE's. Initially a skeptic, Dr. Moody eventually supported medical professionals, hospice workers, and the general public in the subject of near death experiences. An author, speaker, and counselor, he's heard thousands of testimonies. I was once at an event where I saw a man who looked like Raymond Moody. It turns out it wasn't him, but it was exciting to think about being in the same room with the gentle icon whose work I greatly respect.

As a youngster, when I found a book on near death experiences, it felt as if I were holding a sacred treasure. A bridge to the other side! I'm happy this subject is now readily available to the general public. Do you know anyone who's had an experience? Maybe you?

> As a youngster, when I found a book on near death experiences, it felt as if I were holding a sacred treasure. A bridge to the other side!

Keep in mind that there will be people's accounts that remain unspoken due to societal stigma. Resuscitating people is a technology that has improved over the years, so it is no wonder that NDE's have become more of a discussed topic.

In today's world, we have credible experts, such as cardiac surgeons, publicly recognizing NDE's. Cardiac doctor Dr. Lloyd Rudy is one such surgeon. He's shared an account of one patient who died on the surgery table—without bodily function for nearly 20 minutes. This patient who ultimately lived was able to describe details of the hospital scene long after his "death." Dr. Rudy has mentioned that colleagues in his field confirmed similar experiences. Dr. Jeffrey Long, also in medicine, founded the Near Death Experience Research Foundation (NDERF) in 1998. This organization offers numerous resources and has compiled archives of thousands of near death cases.

While near death experiences are unique to each person's situation, common themes are reported. One of my friends told me of being in an ambulance when his heart stopped. Like several NDE's, he experienced being outside of his body. In observation, he said he was traveling above the ambulance.

There have even been accounts of individuals reporting particular objects or people who were well outside of their NDE event—for example, observing someone outside of their room. A patient might describe specific hospital machinery, notes, or tools in a place they were never physically conscious.

In recent years, I had my own NDE. During a legal Ayahuasca journey, I had an uncommon reaction. I was overly sensitive to the plant brew. Unusual to Ayahuasca experiences, I was throwing up days after the event. Individuals onsite reported that I was one of few people in ten years that hit the floor in a state of trauma. My throat was closing up; my hands and lips went numb. I was cold—indescribably cold. I could see myself in my mind's eye with greenish-greyish sweat-beaded skin. My weakened heart palpitated as I strained to breathe. I wavered in and out of consciousness.

In this state, my spirit guides showed up. They conferred about how I'd had too much of the substance for my body. I saw my cloud-like self floating in space-like nothingness. And then I saw *The Light*. It first caught my eye with a beaming flash of radiance. As I write this, I get teary recalling its beauty. Captivated, I floated slowly toward *The Light*—reaching to go into its magnificence.

Other people's NDE accounts include seeing a tunnel and a white light. Often *The Light* is described as being alluring, beyond imagination. To me, *The Light* was HOME. I wanted only to go into the beaming rays. Nothing else mattered. Here, I felt the vastness of EVERYTHING. Timeless, weightless, and in unattached bliss—it was the exquisite essence of LOVE. Intelligently so. For me, I could not get to *The Light* quickly enough. I felt my soul-body slowly reaching and striving toward bliss.

Then a being appeared. It put up what felt like a black energetic brick wall to block *The Light*. The gatekeeper-like entity felt masculine and warrior-like. It swiftly turned my energy away from the direction of *The Light* while it said with the utmost authority, "It's not your time." It was not an exclamation. It was not a rejection. It was not a denial. It was a truth.

It's common for people to experience a being or beings during an NDE. In my case, the gatekeeper-like being was firm but also loving. People also report being greeted by beings that are affiliated with their spiritual beliefs.

My interpretation of this is that Divine takes on a form of comfort and familiarity. People are often incredibly impacted by the intensity of these connections.

Some report a life review—they see flashes of their life in images and emotions. They're given the opportunity to see their impact on others and the world. I've heard of people being offered the consideration of what they might change in their future.

> It is commonly reported that a NDE is a catalyst to remember to live fully.

Many people report coming back with a new life trajectory. That is, they want to do things differently. Others claim to have a deep sense of *knowing* that there is, indeed, something beyond this life. I am confident this is the case. It is commonly reported that a NDE is a catalyst to remember to live fully.

If you could reframe the way you live your current life, how might that look? Feel free to follow up any of these exercises with journaling or reflection. Let's explore:

75. Exploration—Your Own Life Review

If you were to die and look back on your life thus far, what would you have done differently? Doing so is not aimed to bring sadness or shame—approach this as an observer. Can you energetically offer forgiveness to someone, including yourself? Have particularly challenging situations been a catalyst to better things?

In contemplation, what if Divine grace said that in moments, your life would begin anew? If you were to return from an NDE today, how would you want to proceed with your life? Are you currently living and loving fully? Moving forward, what life-essence within *you* do you want to shine in the world?

76. Exploration—Your Gifts in the World

What if you knew, beyond a shadow of a doubt, that there's something more? What if you genuinely experienced the pureness of love, light, and infinite energy—beyond human existence? Are there aspects of your light that you have kept hidden? Are there talents you've not shared with the world as of yet? Close your eyes and reflect. Starting today, is there a new way you'd like to approach life?

77. Exploration—Reflecting Life in Love and Gratitude

The high vibration of love and gratitude are recurring themes throughout this book. Both ignite intuition. Focus on a real, imaginary, or virtual candle flame and be mesmerized by the dancing light. Take a few minutes to feel love and gratitude—enjoy the taste of this raised vibration. Now, consider your answers from the two previous exercises. How would you move forward if today was a fresh start? Are you ready to welcome your intuitive superpowers into this world?

Summary

From out-of-body observations to spiritual beings and life reviews—near death experiences alter life trajectories. As we consider near death experiences, I ask you, "If your life began anew, how would you live it?"

> As we consider near death experiences, I ask you, "If your life began anew, how would you live it?"

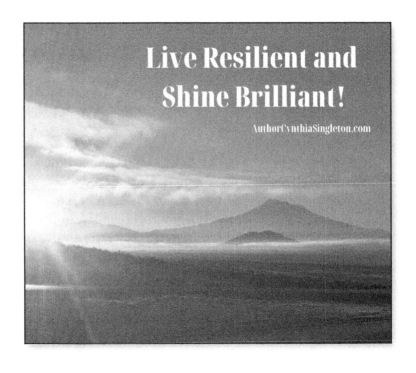

Afterword
The Miraculous Awe of it All

Imagine—picture earth from a distance. Now, look closer. And closer. Feel the breath of our planet's magnificent creatures—see the gaze from behind a Caribou's frozen eyelashes, feel an elephant's deliberate dusty step, and marvel at a dolphin's sleek magnificence. Sip the fragrance of nature's majesty—like honeysuckle to a hummingbird.

Now tune into our human race. Feel the tremendous capacity for love—from belly laughing with a beloved to playfully connecting with our children and pets. Can you see the beauty in the simple acts of kindness that impact our fellow beings?

Imagine the incredible amount of collective miracles that must take place on this planet. We live in immense possibilities—including in our own capacity. When I look from afar, I find it

> When I look from afar, I find it easy to see—humanity's intuitive potential is awakening, and we are invited to participate!

135

easy to see—humanity's intuitive potential is awakening, and we are invited to participate!

> My theory is that we can tune into our gifts like the turn of a water faucet. When deliberate with our intention, we increase the flow of our intuition.

My theory is that we can tune into our gifts like the turn of a water faucet. When deliberate with our intention, we increase the flow of our intuition. We are born with innate abilities. A world awaits. What would it feel like to shine? I celebrate the power of your energetic magnitude.

This book is for you, your loved ones—and for humanity. I encourage you to go back to the parts of this book that intuitively call to you. Perhaps you'd like to implement the goal of focusing on one activity per week. Maybe pick three explorations to try for a month at a time. Open up to random pages for fun and see what captures your attention. What inspires you? What ignites you?

> Your intuition is a sacred gift. I invite you to continue the journey— and play!

We are miraculous. I celebrate the capacity to bring our gifts to life. Spirit and Divine support our path of discovery. Your intuition is a sacred gift. I invite you to continue the journey—and play!

Thank you for your curiosity and courage—for diving into this exciting world of incredible potential. You are a light for this world. We share an awakening path. I'd love to hear about your discoveries, your journey, and your goals at http://www.authorcynthiasingleton.com. Enjoy further explorations. And invite your friends!

Exaltation

Jubilation
Exaltation

A mind's vacation
To check your station

To seek light
In world with plight

Lift your chin
Decide, begin

To follow bliss
Of Divine Kiss

Just reach out
Release your doubt

Make your chance
Learn your dance

Live, love, care…
Cast it everywhere

Cynthia Singleton

About Louie

Whisper an Epic Tale of Magnificent Scale,
With Whiskers Fur and Feline Allure.
—From Cat Whispers by Cynthia Singleton

A bandoned at the door of a small-town library in 2006, Louie Dewey Mocha Latte announced his presence by meowing with "take me home" lungs. A librarian answered this feisty beast's persistence. Coincidentally, this librarian would ultimately become Louie's devoted pet sitter. An incredible connection was bridged. Struck upon meeting, Louie and I were instantaneously smitten.

My feline companion and I shared a magnificent life. My lion and dove, Louie's pitter-pat blissfully echoed through my home. Fetch was a favorite activity of ours. Louie would often set one of his stuffed animals at the door for me as a welcome home gift. With lagoon-blue eyes and soft chinchilla fur, I dubbed his facial markings his "pet me here" place. He was very creative in play and loved crumpled paper and empty boxes. Louie had a culinary flair for cat-friendly foods, including fruits and vegetables. When I'd write, Louie would loyally rest beside me in what I called his "penguin stance." My left shoulder was his perch for shared walks and to dance.

Though often quiet, Louie had signature sounds when playful and happy. I often sang ditties and song snippets to Louie. A favorite was our version of *You Are My Sunshine*. It wasn't until long after his death that I realized a connection—like our song, my current kitty bears the name Sunshine.

Years after Louie's death, in deep meditation, I stood at Divine's feet. I was shown a sleeping light-soul that would soon be my next kitty cat. Mentally, I was invited to request what I would want in my new companion. Sunshine entered my life in 2017. Sunshine bears many of Louie's traits, with an extra sprinkle of cuddly sweetness. Like the song, she makes me happy—each and every day.

Louie continues to leave his signature Divine calling cards of feathers and cat whiskers in life's profound moments.

Made in the USA
Coppell, TX
12 April 2023

15495012R00089